Not Just Paper

If you give God your first and your best, He will bless the rest

Not Just Paper

Principles for Financial Success

Dr. Chonta T. A. Haynes

Copyright © 2018 by Dr. Chonta T. A. Haynes.

ISBN: 978-0-9991733-2-9   eBook

ISBN: 978-0-9991733-3-6   Paperback

All rights reserved. No portion of this eBook or Paperback may be reproduced, stored in a retrieval system, or transmitted in any form or by any means – electronic, mechanical, photocopy, recording, scanning, or other – except for brief quotations in critical reviews or articles, without the prior written permission of the copyright owner.

Unless otherwise indicated, all Scriptural quotations are from the *Authorized Version* of *The Holy Bible: King James Version*. (1995). (electronic ed. of the 1769 edition of the 1611 Authorized Version). All rights reserved.

Scriptural references marked KJV are from *The Holy Bible, King James Version* ®KJV® Copyright © 2004, 1986, 1983 by Thomas Nelson, Inc. All rights reserved.

Scriptural references marked AMP are from the *Amplified Bible*®, Copyright © 1954, 1958, 1962, 1964, 1965, 1987 by The Lockman Foundation. All rights reserved.

Scriptural references marked Wuest are taken from *The New Testament: An Expanded Translation*, Copyright © 1994, 1961 by Wm. B. Eerdmans Publishing Co., Grand Rapids, MI. All rights reserved.

Scriptural references marked NIV are taken from the *Holy Bible, New International Version* ®NIV ® Copyright © 1973, 1978, 1984 by the International Bible Society. Used by permission of Zondervan Publishing House. All rights reserved.

This book was printed in the United States of America.

To order additional copies in any format, contact:

Heart 2 Heart Truth Ministries, LLC

1-813-299-2742

www.ChontaHaynes.com   H2HTruth.org

https://youtube.com/@ChontaHaynes

Other Books by Dr. Chonta T. A. Haynes:

Financial Wisdom For Financial Freedom

Family Worship: Reaching All Who Attend

Divinely Connected: Steps to Fearless Financial Freedom

Divinely Connected: Praying through life's struggles

Divinely Connected: Sister 2 Sister

Destined To Prosper: Align Your Biblical Financial Personality with Strategies to Build Wealth and Abundance

Table of Contents

Introduction 1
Chapter 1: God's Design 7
Chapter 2: Money Test 19
    Work Ethic Test 20
    Self-Control Test 22
    Integrity Money Test 24
    Love For People Money Test 26
    Love For God Money Test 29
Chapter 3: Abundant Living 33
    Poverty vs. Prosperity 34
Chapter 4: Coming out of Poverty 43
    Binding the Enemy 46
    Dispatch Ministering Angels 50
    Divine Summons 53
    Work of the Hand 56
    Godly Wisdom 58
Chapter 5: Going onto Abundance 65
Chapter 6: Scriptural Ways to Achieve Abundance 75
    Onward to Abundance 85
    Limitations 103
Chapter 7: Covenant 107
    Tithing 109
    The Principle of the Tithe 110

The Law of the Tithe 125
The Grace of the Tithe 146
Chapter 8: Summarizing – The Children of Israel's Journey 161
- Spiritual 164
- Business 169
- View of God 171
- Motivation 173

Chapter 9: New Testament Church Giving 175
- God's Purpose for Giving 183
- God's Miracle Provision Reminders: 203
- In God We Trust 210
- Money Test 211
- Abundant Living 219
- Coming out of Poverty 221
- Going onto Abundance 223
- Scriptural Ways to Achieve Abundance 225
- Covenant 233
- Summarizing the Journey 234
- New Testament Giving 235

Introduction

When it comes to the subject of money, a multitude of thoughts begin dancing around in our heads. A free-flowing fountain that never ends. That money tree mom said wasn't real. Handcuffs on our wallets jacked by greedy grabbers. Nightmares of hands coming out of nowhere, palms open asking, no begging to take what we envision we need. It's a subject near and dear to our wallets that affect our hearts. If we are honest, how we handle money is a mirror of our heart and a string tied to what we love. Can it cause damage? What does it say about you based on how much you have, spend and give? What about your relationship with God as it relates to how you view money and give it away?

The Bible has a lot to say about money. Jesus had a lot to say about money. He said it was a little matter; minor compared to other issues. So, why does it take up so much of our thought real estate and affect our lives in ways we can't imagine? It is something we use every day, and something of value. Putting it in proper perspective is the key to a right relationship with God and financial freedom.

Starting with our relationship with God, in His eyes money is Not Just Paper. We will also find out God's will for us as identified in the Bible. Will we acknowledge Him? Will we be obedient to the Word? Will we obtain the level of prosperity He desires? Will we cut the string to our wallet and release the treasures? There is a God idea of abundance and benefits to covenant.

Money is a test; a test of our work ethic, self-control, integrity, love for people and love for God. Delving deep into Scripture and then looking practically at our lives we discover that what we have in our wallets is Not Just Paper. It defines our relationship with God and with others. Prayerfully we will be better stewards by the completion of this book, hearts open and minds renewed.

God had a plan for us to live in abundance. After all, Jesus died for us, according to John 10:10, to live an abundant life. With so great a sacrifice, an all-in proposition, why dear heart are we not walking in it? What blockage is there that keeps the river of abundance from flowing freely? Do you have faith in God? Is He your supply? Do you know what He desires for you? Are you a reservoir or a funnel? Abundant living involves us having not only our needs met but having excess in which to give to the Lord and to sow. We find that our giving affords a multitude of benefits and money is Not Just Paper.

A covenant relationship is made by the stronger party who also mandates the terms. Because the Almighty creator of the Universe offers us a covenant relationship where He promises us protection and being our exceeding great reward; ideally, we would jump at being obedient. Why aren't we submissive? Do we know the awesome promises of the covenant and the why of our giving? Our obedience is a reflection of our love for God and the fact that money is Not Just Paper.

And so, our journey begins. We start with prayer, a Bible, an open heart ready for a trip from heaven through history to health. Deep breath... let's ask for divine guidance, wisdom, refreshing of the mind and the abundant life promised!

Most Gracious and heavenly Father we do thank you, bless and honor you for who You are. We thank you that every good and every perfect gift comes from you. You are our source and we give you preeminence. There is none like You and with You all things are possible. We acknowledge your divine will and your awesome plans for us.

We thank you Lord that the things that we are going to learn, the theology as well the practical application is going to elevate us to a new level. We thank you for a spirit of giving and that we will walk in abundance. We thank you that you died for us to have an abundant life here on earth even before we get to heaven. So, we're thanking you in advance for how you are going to open our minds, open our hearts, open our pockets, open every prison door that has us bound so that we will walk out free. Give us wisdom to handle our finances and get them in order. Help us to climb out of debt and set our plans to follow your ways. We ask for guidance as we begin our journey. Direct our steps because you promised to light our path. Refresh our minds and help us to renew it so that we walk in abundance.

Forgive us of debts we have not prioritized and paid in the past. Forgive us of trivializing others we owe. You said we are wicked if we don't pay our debts so we ask that you give us opportunity to rectify the situation and bridge the connectiveness again. We ask for grace and favor as we get back on track.

We desire Lord to let our lights shine so that others will see Your work in our lives and glorify You. Our desire is that your Kingdom come on this earth and that Your will be done. Help us be examples for others to follow and bring glory to Your name.

In all the abundance of Jesus' wonderful name we do pray and give you thanks. Amen.

Chapter 1: God's Design

When it comes to the subject of finances mixed with Biblical principles blank stares emerge. The thought of the reverential posture of what the Word says, God's design, juxtaposed to what we want to do causes consternation. We sometimes don't walk like the obedient servants we claim. As we cover the theology, the theory and practical applications, it is my prayer that God divinely intervenes and speaks to your heart so that you can walk in abundance. Where are you in relation to what God said? Why are you afraid to follow God's principles? What hinders you? What do you really want? How can you obtain God's desire? How much more of His promises will you receive? These questions allow for intimate relationship with the Father. As children, we sit at His feet to listen and learn. Father teach us to trust you!

Secondarily my objective is to establish you firmly in the true Word of God concerning finances and God's Kingdom that you live in provision and abundance to God's glory and lead others to the same place of liberty and victory. The next phase is to be the example for others. Knowing, then doing, leading to showing is the goal. God set the plan in motion and had Jesus demonstrate it clearly. He said, He illustrated and the disciples replicated.

> DISCIPLE — a student, learner, or pupil. In the Bible the word is used most often to refer to a follower of Jesus. The word is rarely used in the Old Testament. Isaiah used the term "disciples" to refer to those who are taught or instructed (Is. 8:16).
>
> *Nelson's new illustrated Bible dictionary.* Nashville, TN: Thomas Nelson, Inc.

> **FAITH — trusting, relying and depending upon God giving credence to His word.**

We begin by recognizing that as disciples of the Lord we stand ready to be submissive to His word, His will and His ways. Because we have faith, our desire once we know God's word is to be obedient and therefore right in the center of His divine will. We need to know His word which reveals His will as it concerns us and finances. We start off with the fact that God gives life itself, eternal life and all good things that pertain to life.

"And the LORD God formed man of the dust of the ground, and breathed into his nostrils the breath of life; and man became a living soul." (Genesis 2:7)

You would think it is common sense that of course God created the heavens and the earth. Proof one – God's word tells us so. If we believe God's word is divinely inspired and is direct from His lips then we take stock in what it says. It is the inerrant (without error), infallible (it cannot fail), and inspired (God breathed) word. The book of Genesis records for us the creation story. Within it everything was set in motion and designed to be sustainable. The sun and moon were set. The seas and lands were established. The vegetation and animals created. Then God created man (Adam). Creationists believing the account of the Bible attribute all the intricate details to an intelligent designer – God – who with all knowledge set the trajectory. Life began.

As an aside, there are those that subscribe to the Big Bang Theory which is an effort to explain the beginning of our universe. It states that an infinitesimally small, infinitely hot, infinitely dense something – a singularity- appeared and after its appearance it inflated, expanded and cooled until all that we now see – earth, sky, animals, humans- were instantly created. One comment and I will leave it for the apologists – Where did this singularity originate? It cries for an intelligent designer to order and create all the intricate detailed systems we enjoy. (See Genesis 1:1-27; Isaiah 45:5-12, 18; Ephesians 3:9; and Colossians 1:16)

"In the beginning was the Word, and the Word was with God, and the Word was God. The same was in the beginning with God. All things were made by him; and without him was not any thing made that was made. In him was life; and the life was the light of men." (John 1:1-4) God created the heavens and the earth and breathed life into man. God's breathing into man allowed man to come alive (physically). He was no longer mere clay; unable to have activity of his limbs, breath, reasoning, speaking, etc. God created life so He is the giver of life itself (physical). It is declared in the beginning that the Divine Creator set out to make things that were "good and very good". *"And God saw everything that He had made, and, behold, it was very good. And the evening and the morning were the sixth day." (Genesis 1:31)*

"This is the record that God had given to us eternal life and this life is in His Son. He that hath the Son has life. He that has not the Son of God hath not life these things have I written unto you that believe on the name of the Son of God that you may know that you have eternal life and that you may believe on the name of the Son of God. This is the confidence that we have in Him that if we ask anything according to His will He hears us and if we know that He hears us whatsoever we ask we know that we have the petition that we desired of Him". (1 John 5:11-15)

Man is a three part being; spirit, soul and body (1 Thessalonians 5:23). As God created Adam in his original state all three parts were alive. The Greek word *soma* identifies the physical body. If we have breath we are physically alive and our bodies function. The Greek word *psuche* references our soul which is comprised of our mind, will and emotions. Our personality; thought process, volition and temperament demonstrates life also in an individual. The third part of man, the *pneuma* meaning breath, is the spiritual. Man died spiritually as a result of the fall (Genesis 2:17). The original intent was for man to have a continual relationship with God communing daily and receiving blessings from that union. In order for a reinstatement of that connection God had to make provision for redemption to the state of full life and this was achieved through Jesus Christ. If we believe in the Son accepting His sacrifice and acknowledging Him as Lord and Savior, we are born again; spiritually alive. This life because of our relationship with the Son (Jesus Christ) is eternal; lasts forever. If we don't believe in the Son, eternal damnation awaits; spiritual death remains. Not only did God breathe physical life into Adam including his soul but because of Jesus we are quickened (made alive) spiritually allowing for eternal life. In Ephesians 2:8, the Bible says that **"for by grace you are saved through faith and not of yourselves it is the gift of God"**. God gives us wonderful gifts and the greatest is the gift of salvation. We are saved, *sode-zo* in the Greek which means we are rescued and delivered. It's by His grace, God's unmerited favor, it's His divine supernatural ability that He has added to us so that influence is not only in the heart of man but it shows up in our life as we go forward. We are then rescued from the penalty of sin and the wrath of God. The Bible records that the wages of sin is death but the gift of God is eternal life (Romans 6:23). This death because of sin is spiritual death. Putting our faith in God rescues us from this eternal spiritual death and affords deliverance from our natural tendencies. We are then delivered through our trust, our reliance and our dependence on Him and it is not based on what we have done but it is a gift from God. Deliverance from sin which entered at the fall of man and translation into the Kingdom of God came with our spiritual awakening (Colossians 1:13). Eternal life with God is available for all who accept. God not only gives life itself (physical life) and eternal life (spiritual life) but He gives all good things that pertain to life.

SAVED
4982 ἐκσώζω, σώζω [sozo /sode·zo/]
1 to save, keep safe and sound, to rescue from danger or destruction. 1a one (from injury or peril). to save a suffering one (from perishing), i.e. one suffering from disease, to make well, heal, restore to health. to preserve one who is in danger of destruction, to save or rescue. 1b to save in the technical biblical sense. negatively. to deliver from the penalties of the Messianic judgment. to save from the evils which obstruct the reception of the Messianic deliverance.
Strong, J. (1995). <u>Enhanced Strong's Lexicon.</u> <u>Woodside Bible Fellowship.</u>

James 1:17 states, *"Every good gift and every perfect gift is from above, and cometh down from the Father of lights, with whom is no variableness, neither shadow of turning" (KJV).* It says every good (*agathós*- benevolent, profitable, useful, excellent, virtuous, upright) gift (*dosis* – the act of giving) and every perfect (*téleios* – complete, full, wanting nothing, one that has the necessary qualities) gift (*dórēma* – the result of the act of giving) is going to come from God. When we see cometh in the King James, it is a present participle meaning that it keeps on coming. It's a constant flow with recurring action. Let's consider this: If every good gift and every perfect gift constantly comes down from heaven it's as if it keeps raining on us if we would but pay attention. The thought reminds me of the Barney song that says, "If all the raindrops were lemon drops and gum drops, Oh what a rain that would be... standing outside with my mouth open wide..." Imagine opening wide to receive all that God is pouring out. Take a moment lift your hands to heaven and receive the rain and refreshing; drink in the awesomeness of God being present in your life and be aware of the profitable, useful, and complete gifts He sends. If we think in those terms then we won't just hold onto some of the purposeful gifts that He has been giving to us. We will become good stewards and sow into others recognizing our blessings and abundance. He keeps raining down favor; we say I'm expecting something good to happen to me today. How is it going to happen? It will come from God. I'm expecting something good to happen through me because He has already rained on me and I can rain on somebody else. God is the fountain and Father of all good. Let me say it again, every good gift comes down in a constant flow from the Father of lights. God is Light. In the beginning God said, "let there be light" (Genesis 1:3). Jesus as He walked the earth said, "I am the light of the world" (John 8:12). He also said, "You are the light of the world", you need to go and shine forth in darkness (Matthew 5:14-16). Recognizing that light dispels all darkness we are to shine in every area including finances. He has given us these great gifts and they continue to come down and He is the light. God is emanating light. He is holy and there is no unholiness in Him; that's what is meant by no variableness, no shadow of turning, no darkness at all. God is the same in His nature and influence; He is unchangeable. Every good act of giving (*dosis*) and every perfect gift (*dórēma*) is from above. We ascribe to Him all the benefits which we have. Rest in the unchangeable Lord of light and rely on His life-giving Word of Truth (Ephesians 1:13)

All good things God has given, it's His character and His nature. Every good gift and every perfect gift comes from Him and continuously flows from Him. A part of the good things includes riches {*ashar*}. When God gives riches, gifts or treasures He adds no sorrow; deep distress, sadness, regret, resultant unhappy or unpleasant state.

RICHES
6238 עָשַׁר [ʿashar /aw·shar/]
1 to be or become rich or wealthy, enrich, pretend to be rich. 1a to be or become rich. 1b to make rich. to gain riches. 1c to enrich oneself, pretend to be rich.

Strong, J. (1995). *Enhanced Strong's Lexicon*. Woodside Bible Fellowship.

SORROW
6089 עֶצֶב, עָצָב [ʿetseb /eh·tseb/]
1 pain, hurt, toil, sorrow, labour, hardship. 1a pain. 1b hurt, offense. 1c toil, hardship.

Strong, J. (1995). *Enhanced Strong's Lexicon*. Woodside Bible Fellowship.

"The blessing of the Lord, it maketh rich, And he addeth no sorrow with it." (Proverbs 10:22)

That is a promise from God that we should stand on. God gives the gifts and the ability to enjoy them. That's good news and a great God that loves us enough to protect the gifts from causing us grief and heartache.

So, what is God's will? God wants us to be in communion with Him which necessitates a spiritual life. He wants us to have everlasting life with Him. He wants to favor us. He wants to give us profitable gifts. He wants to give us gifts that has the necessary qualities on a regular basis. Let's look at 2 Peter 1:2-3.

ABASED
5013 ταπεινόω [tapeinoo /tap·i·no·o/]
1 to make low, bring low. 1a to level, reduce to a plain. 1b metaph. to bring into a humble condition, reduce to meaner circumstances. to assign a lower rank or place to. to abase. to be ranked below others who are honoured or rewarded. to humble or abase myself by humble living. 1c to lower, depress. of one's soul bring down one's pride. to have a modest opinion of one's self. to behave in an unassuming manner. devoid of all haughtines

Strong, J. (1995). <u>Enhanced Strong's Lexicon.</u> <u>Woodside Bible Fellowship.</u>

ABOUND
4052 περισσεύω [perisseuo /per·is·syoo·o/]
1 to exceed a fixed number of measure, to be left over and above a certain number or measure. 1a to be over, to remain. 1b to exist or be at hand in abundance. to be great (abundant). a thing which comes in abundance, or overflows unto one, something falls to the lot of one in large measure. to redound unto, turn out abundantly for, a thing. 1c to abound, overflow. to be abundantly furnished with, to have in abundance, abound in (a thing), to be in affluence. to be pre-eminent, to excel. to excel more than, exceed. 2 to make to abound. 2a to furnish one richly so that he has abundance. 2b to make abundant or excellent.

Strong, J. (1995). <u>Enhanced Strong's Lexicon.</u> <u>Woodside Bible Fellowship.</u>

"Grace and peace be multiplied unto you through the knowledge of God, and of Jesus our Lord, According as his divine power hath given unto us all things that pertain unto life and godliness, through the knowledge of him that hath called us to glory and virtue"

The Apostle Peter wishes multiplication and increase of divine favor, the work of grace in them, and that peace with God may abound to them. This comes by the acknowledging and believing in God and Jesus and is a great improvement of spiritual life, or it could not be the way to life eternal (John 17:3). The more you know, the more you are going to be increased with grace and peace. He says this divine power gives us all things. All things! That little word ALL is including everything. Just like the good and perfect gifts and all things that pertain to life, God is giving it to us. Nothing is left out! The Scripture records that the Bible has everything in it pertaining to life and godliness. Godliness is our reverence, our respect, our piety towards God. Peter records that everything is in the book and it is based on you digging out those treasures, getting that knowledge, getting that understanding and walking it out in wisdom. So, since God is giving us all of this... He calls us to glory and virtue. The word virtue here is excellence. God is calling us to financial excellence. There's a quality of excellence that needs to follow our lives. According to God's will for us we're supposed to be living an abundant life. If we recognize that His word has everything that we need and we seek it and we follow... Jesus said if you love me you will obey my commandments (John 15:10). If we follow what He says then every good gift will follow. We will not only have life but also eternal life. Because we are seeking Him and we are following Him, we will have this great abundant life now and yes, we don't have to wait until we get to heaven but we will take a lot of people with us. It is just that good! We will see it overflowing in our life. God's desire or His will is going to cover life, eternal life and all good things that pertain to life.

So, In God we trust? Trust speaks of an assured reliance on and to place confidence in something or someone. When we truly trust God, our confidence and our reliance is in Him coming through and not our working it out. The giver of life, the preserver of life, and the gifter in life is God. His word tells us of His will, **"For I know the thoughts that I think toward you, saith the LORD, thoughts of peace, and not of evil, to give you an expected end."** *(Jeremiah 29:11)* Knowing that God has a great plan for us allows us to confidently rely on Him working on our behalf. Where are you? Are you ready to be tested?

In God We Trust
Bible Study
Page 210

Chapter 2: Money Test

All through school you have been given opportunities to show what you know. We call them tests. When they present themselves in everyday life we get a glimpse of our makeup. Sometimes we like the results and sometimes we realize the test requires a retake. The good news is that with God there are retakes and no failures.

Money is a matter that is linked to our heart with a string tied to our wallets. There are several tests we take with money; the ultimate is how we act when we are abased – having little- and when we abound – having much. The Apostle Paul records for us that he learned to be content in whichever state he found himself (Philippians 4:12). For now, as a check along the way, we will discuss money as a test of our: work ethic; self-control; integrity; love for people and love for God.

Work Ethic Test

"For even when we were with you, this we commanded you, that if any would not work, neither should he eat."
(2 Thessalonians 3:10)

The Bible says that a man (or woman) that doesn't work doesn't eat (2 Thessalonians 3:10). It carries that if there is no effort in sustaining yourself, there will be nothing which to be sustained. Often when there is no income the false expectation is that someone else will provide. As Christians we, with a heart like God, want to reach out and help those in need. The sad truth is that there are those – con artists- that prey on the goodness of others. There are also those with an entitlement mentality that believe they are owed and have a right to what belongs to someone else. And there is the covetous spirited individual that cries out like Robin Hood – steal from the rich and give to the poor (only because they are not rich and not fighting for injustice).

God gives us the power to get wealth (Deuteronomy 8:18). He gives us the ability, coupled with our efforts to make a living to support ourselves. That income or salary determines how much you have to spend, give and save. This doesn't mean you won't fall on hard times. It doesn't mean that extenuating circumstances won't put you in a predicament that requires temporary assistance. The point is, if we are trusting God we will do what He has given us the ability to do and we will see the manifestation of Him coming through.

Your willingness to work and how you work are both test areas. Do you give an honest days work for an honest days pay? Are you in on time and work all 8 hours? Do you leave early, goof off or use the phone for personal business during working hours? Would you higher you? Are you an excellent employee or business owner? Are you paying your employees fair wages? Are they paid on time?

The idea of the test is that in the Kingdom we are ultimately employed by the King of Kings. If every day you approached your job as if Jesus is your boss, what actions would you do differently? If you were to run your company knowing Jesus was looking over the books and the management, how would you lead differently?

The parable of the workers is excellent to make this point (Matthew 20:1-16). Some workers were hired at the beginning of the day and some at the end. It didn't matter when they came into employment the key was they were willing, they each gave their best and they each got paid. Now many would focus on the manager paying them differently but for our money test we will concentrate on their willingness and their excellence in service.

How do you work when you think you are underpaid or undervalued? After you agreed to the pay, are you disgruntled and take (steal) supplies because they don't pay you enough anyway? Are you rebellious and combative because you've allowed offense, covetousness or bitterness to enter your heart? Do you have faith in God's faithfulness?

"And whatsoever ye do, do it heartily, as to the Lord, and not unto men" (Colossians 3:23)

Self-Control Test

The Apostle Paul in Philippians 4 said he learned to be abased and to abound. Many times, the biggest issue is the abounding more so than the abasement. Some of us are better at surviving in famine than we are living in blessing. When we have a lot of money our hearts are tested whether we become that reservoir and hold onto every penny. This is illustrated in the man who built barns (Luke 12:16-21). He was successful and had amassed significant gains. As he kept adding to his worldly riches he was forced to need a larger place to store his wealth. The unfortunate issue is that the monetary success superseded his spiritual growth. He didn't make the time to ensure his eternal destination was heaven. He may have also forsaken relationships, there is no mention of family or friends. His idea was gaining the whole world in the process he lost his soul. Tomorrow isn't promised but we are still blessed to be a blessing. When we have much, one test is whether we will help those in need and share with others.

Another test of having much is not only the propensity to selfishness but also lavishly spending. If there is no plan for what comes in and what goes out (read budget) there is the high probability that more will be spent than you have. Ask the many winners of the lottery. In most cases they are broke today. If you never learn to handle money, throwing more money at a situation only exacerbates the problem. Over spending is a part of the self-control test.

Priorities come into question as it relates to money and spending. The overall idea would be to give some, save some and spend some. The God we serve is a generous God. He lavishly blesses us giving us new mercies every day. He provides rain to water the grass, sunshine to warm us, and He even through touching the hearts of others has them give to us. In the book of James, he reminds us that if we see our brother who doesn't dress like we do, to not treat them differently (James 2:1-9). He goes on to remind us that if our brother doesn't have, we shouldn't withhold assistance when we have it to give (James 2:15-16). In the book of Acts as the believers of 'The Way' gathered, they had all things in common (Acts 2:44-47). They provided and shared with one another. Over and over the Word pricks our hearts to loose the string attached to our wallets and be generous givers.

The question is, what are you seeking? Are you looking to build the bigger barns and forsake earthly relationships and eternal life? Are you overspending? If retail therapy is your outlet, ask yourself what motivates you to spend? Are you generous with the blessings of God? Are you storing up treasures in heaven where moth and rust can't destroy (Matthew 6:19-21)? Where your treasure is, there your heart will be also.

Integrity Money Test

Integrity is defined as the quality of being honest and having strong moral principles; ethical uprightness. It also brings with it the connotation of being whole and undivided; not one way at home and another at church. When it comes to finances, the Bible is clear that we deal honestly with both our brothers and sisters in Christ and the world.

Psalm 37:21 says, *"The wicked borroweth, and payeth not again: but the righteous sheweth mercy, and giveth."* We have the responsibility that if we charged or ate or agreed to purchase something, we complete the transaction. Not paying for a service is like robbing the individual of their time, effort and intellectual property. Receiving an item, using it then deciding you want to return it is equivalent to stealing from that business owner. They not only paid for the item but now can't sell it at full price. You've cheated them out of their livelihood.

Who is your Father? If it is God, then your actions should be patterned after His. Let your yes be yes and your no, no (James 5:12). You should swear to your own hurt and change not (Psalm 15:4). If you commit to something then follow through. If you sign an agreement, complete the terms.

The idea of trying to get over on someone taking advantage of them is a test of integrity. Are you operating on moral principles or are you being manipulative, deceptive and selfish?

Integrity at the root deals with character. Character is the mental and moral qualities distinctive to an individual. Money tests your character in how you act because you have it and what you do to get it. The fruit of the spirit should be evident in the life of the believer (Galatians 5:22-25). These qualities should develop as we continue working out our souls (mind, will, and emotions) salvation (Philippians 2:12). The influx of money should not effect our treatment of others negatively.

Will you pay what you owe in a timely fashion? Will you prioritize your debt over personal desires? Will you keep your word? How do your friends and business associates view you as it relates to money? Are you afraid to ask them?

We have beliefs and thoughts about money. The question becomes, who told you that? The key is that whatever our thoughts are, they should line up with God's word and our beliefs should follow. If they don't line up with the Word, then our minds need to be renewed (Romans 12:2). Our desire should be to please God and that involves knowing His word and being obedient (Luke 6:46).

Love For People Money Test

"For ye have the poor always with you; but me ye have not always." (Matthew 26:11, Mark 14:7, John 12:8) Jesus in his conversation with His disciples rebuked them because of their disdain for the sacrifice being offered to Him. Yes, there is a need to give to those who are less fortunate. There will be those who fall on hard times and need assistance temporarily. There will be aging parents that need the help of their children (1 Timothy 5:8). There will be those you should just want to bless.

Our response to others reflects our heart. Sometimes we have pity or compassion and our feet remain fixed. The Bible says faith without works is dead (James 2:17). If we trust God to meet our needs and He puts someone in our path whose needs are great, don't you think He would supply enough to meet theirs too? You may say, they can have their own faith to get out of their situation. They could, but what if God is testing that string tied to your wallet? Imagine Him playing it like a guitar. How many chords does He have to play for you to be moved with compassion? What specifically pulls enough that you release what He has given you the power to get? Can He trust that if He gets the money to you that you will release it when He asks?

This love for people shows up in the other tests already identified as well. The Bible states that to whom much is given, much is required (Luke 12:48). There is a demand or expectation that whatever has been given by God that we would be good stewards – managers of that which belongs to someone else. God gives us all things richly to enjoy (1 Timothy 6:17). We have the responsibility to appropriate it according to His principles. We can't take it with us and we also must give account (1 Timothy 6:7; Matthew 25:14-30). It is also identified in Luke's gospel that if we aren't good stewards over a little, we won't be over much (Luke 16:10-13). Often someone declares that they would give a large contribution to the church when they win the lottery or a million dollars. The truth is the same thought process you have about money with a little is the same pattern you would follow with a lot. It's easier to renew your mind while you have a manageable amount so that the true riches can be given later. God gives us what we can handle! Prove that you can be a good steward over little and He will give you the abundance to handle.

In Galatians 6:10 the Bible records, *"As we have therefore opportunity, let us do good unto all men, especially unto them who are of the household of faith."* Upon careful study and within context, this passage refers to how we give to those in service in the church. They can be leaders or lay people, those working for the Kingdom should not always do so without compensation. How do you feel about paying the Pastor, leaders, office staff, cleaning crew? Does it line up with God's economy and Him being the inheritance for the Levites? (more later in the book on this subject) Renewing the mind may be in order but

STEWARDSHIP — the management of another person's property, finances, or household affairs. As far as Christians are concerned, stewardship involves the responsibility of managing God's work through the church. God has appointed all Christians to be His stewards on earth. Stewardship is not an option, as Paul points out about his own call. Being a steward is a necessary part of believing the gospel, even if it involves sacrificing personal rewards (1 Cor. 9:17).
As the parable of the talents (Matt. 25:14–30) shows, Christians will be held accountable for the way in which they manage God's affairs as stewards. These matters include extending the church's ministry through the preaching of the gospel (Col. 1:24–28), supporting the church financially (Acts 4:32–37), and ministering to the sick and needy (Matt. 25:31–46).

Youngblood, R. F., Bruce, F. F., & Harrison, R. K., Thomas Nelson Publishers (Eds.). (1995). In *Nelson's new illustrated Bible dictionary*. Nashville, TN: Thomas Nelson, Inc.

simply use this test to gauge your heart about money. Are you willing to sacrifice for the saints? Sacrificial offering requests for benevolence funds, do you contribute? Are you really making a sacrifice or is it within your plan of giving?

Giving is a part of the money test. This involves not only giving to individuals but also groups, charitable organizations, and the church. Are you a generous giver?

Love For God Money Test

Studying God's word as it relates to giving, convicts on several levels and makes one aware of how money is misperceived. One such illustration that comes to mind has to do with a young woman that was taking a trip. Her normal trip preparation required that she get to the airport early and take a few moments before it was time to board. This allowed for breathing and letting go of all the normal stresses of life. This particular day had some extra challenges so she slipped into the coffee shop and bought a small bag of cookies. This was a treat that she was looking forward to. She sat down in the terminal to read her book before the flight. Only a few moments had passed when she became appalled. The older gentleman sitting next to her began to rip open the bag of cookies. As she heard him she couldn't believe what was happening. How dare he, she thought. Then moments later, he was eating a cookie. The nerve she thought and without putting down her book, she reached down next to her grabbed a cookie and shoved it into her mouth. As she swallowed hard she was suddenly taken aback again. He had reached down and grabbed another cookie and continued eating. 'The nerve of some people', she thought. What is this world coming to? She wasn't going to be out done, so she took another cookie. She soon noticed that the man picked up the last cookie, broke it in half, ate a part and left the other for her. He really has a lot of nerve she thought again but quickly ate the last half. Before she could say anything, the older gentleman got up and boarded another flight. She just couldn't believe what just happened. As she got on her flight still reeling with anger about the encounter, she sat in her seat and positioned herself for the flight. She opened her purse before putting it under the seat in front of her. There in her purse was a small bag of cookies. All the while she thought the older gentleman was eating her cookies, it turned out she was eating his. Her heart sank. (Excerpt from *Keys to Financial Excellence* by Phil Pringle)

The story reminds us of how some misperceive money. We think it belongs to us and we can be very selfish about it like that small bag of cookies. We want to keep it to ourselves and get upset if we think someone else is taking what belongs to us. The truth of the matter is that the older gentleman in the story is a representation of God. He has the cookies and He compassionately shares with us from His bountiful riches. Psalm 24:1 states that the earth is the Lord's and everything in it. He gives us the power to get wealth, yet we perceive incorrectly that when we give He is taking from us. Everything we have God gave it to us and if He asks us to return a small portion to Him it really isn't much that He is requesting.

Are you being selfish holding onto your little bag of cookies without realizing you've been eating God's all along? Did you incorrectly assume that what you were consuming really belonged to the Father? Now that your eyes are opened, what will you do differently? How will you think differently?

Matthew 22:1 says the Kingdom of Heaven is like a King who has a wedding feast. It goes on to say that there were those who were invited to the feast but didn't come. There were others who were then invited which attended but all did not respect the King. One was there without the proper attire. The Bible declares that where two or three are gathered God is in the midst (Matthew 18:20). The King shows up each time we gather together. So, when we enter the house of God and at least one other saint is there, so is God. When we come before Him we should honor Him. He's worthy of honor just because He is the King and it is His Kingdom. As subjects we should bow down always and respect the King.

Only a few verses later Jesus declares render unto Caesar that which is Caesar's and unto God that which is God's (Matthew 22:21; Mark 12:17; Luke 20:25). Why then is it so hard as we come to worship to give God what we should? Every time we enter the house of God we should be prepared to give and be grateful to do so. If the King is present, we should have a present for the King.

The King is all powerful, there is none like Him! He's invincible and adored! He is in control and His kingdom is in order. The King is worthy of honor and He bestows benevolence on all in the Kingdom. It's because of all that He does for us that we have an abundant life. The King protects, provides and plans for our good.

There's another story we are familiar with that reflects on the idea of our love for God; the widow's mite (Mark 12:41-44; Luke 21:1-4). She gave all. She sacrificed. Not only do we give financially but we offer ourselves first to the King. If you are truly all-in then so is your wallet. Notice Jesus was watching the giving. Sometimes we don't consider the fact that He sees when we show up late because our heart isn't to give; we purposely miss offering time. He knows when we argue about what's requested for contributions. He knows when we don't put Him first acknowledging it in our tithe. And just to add an exclamation point to the tithe subject, it should be the first check/gift we give (more on this subject later in the book). If we are honoring God with the first of our substance, we should do it immediately before any other bill is paid (Proverbs 3:9).

The question is, since God gives us so much, how much more should we be willing to give Him?

"Honour the LORD with thy substance, and with the firstfruits of all thine increase: So shall thy barns be filled with plenty, and thy presses shall burst out with new wine."
(Proverbs 3:9,10)

Money Test
Bible Study
Page 211

Chapter 3: Abundant Living

"The thief cometh not, but for to steal, and to kill, and to destroy: I am come that they might have life, and that they might have it more abundantly." (John 10:10)

Jesus died for us to have an abundant life, then why aren't we living it? What is abundant living? What does it look like? Anything promised by God to us is a promise waiting to be claimed. When we get to heaven, surely we don't want to hear that there were a multitude of tangible blessings just waiting that we left on the table. Some unclaimed because we didn't believe, some because we didn't ask and some because we just didn't know it was available. Assuming we start with nothing or very little let's trace through the Bible from poverty through abundance picking up gold nuggets along the way. Let's discover God's ideas, His plans, His will for us and change our thoughts to achieve the life Jesus died for us to have.

Poverty vs. Prosperity

> **POVERTY** — Living in lack and want below the basic needs of life and having nothing of which to give to the Lord.

There is a difference between poverty and prosperity. Erase in your mind any thoughts or any definition you would have of poverty. Living in the United States of America, our definition of what poverty looks like is very different from someone who lives in a third world country. For clarity we will define poverty as living in lack and want below the basic needs of life and having nothing of which to give to the Lord. Basic needs include food, clothes and shelter. This is not talking about a steak dinner or a large house where you have an excess of rooms. And I'm not referring to the latest designer clothes. If you have the basic needs: you have something to eat and it could be just one meal a day; you have some place to lay your head, a place that you are covered from the elements outside; and you have something to put on your body. That's the basic needs. Are you living in lack and want below your basic needs? That's where we will draw the line. Poverty is below the basic needs which are not met and you would have nothing you can give to the Lord.

> **PROSPERITY** — The Grace of God by which we live above lack and want and have a supply beyond of which we can give to the

Prosperity then is the grace of God by which we live above lack and want and have a supply beyond of which we can give to the Lord. Imagine there is a line in the air, the height of say a teenage girl. Prosperity says my basic needs would be the top of her head and I am either right at that line or I am above that line. By this child's standards your basic needs then have been met if your supply reaches the top of her head. We will then have two different levels of prosperity. One is going to be provision and the other abundance. Provision is having just enough; your supply is sufficient but there isn't anything left over. Let's look at Psalm 24:1

"The earth is the Lord's and the fullness thereof, the world and they that dwell therein."

The earth is the Lord's and we all belong to Him. With the definitions we've clarified, we have to understand that most people are not living in poverty. You can have one room or a shack and still not be in poverty if you are eating. It's a different thought process. We will discuss what God calls abundance later. Provision says God has met my needs. If you're in poverty, you can't eat, you can't sleep, you don't have clothes, you have nothing you can give. If you did get a dollar that dollar would need to be used to eat or to buy clothing so that you're not exposed to the elements in order that you still have life. You need to have life and you won't if you don't have enough to live or drink or eat so that's the minimum requirements.

There is a difference between needs and luxuries. Many people have become comfortable with luxuries and call them needs. Internet is not a need. Cell phones are not a need. TV is not a need. Cable is not a need. A phone period is not a need. You don't need those things. In other words, it is not germane for you to have life.

In a third world country many mission organizations go in and set up orphanages and children's homes. They do this so they can feed the children because parents are trying to decide which child to feed since they can't provide for all of them. They don't have their needs met. Unless you are told these stories or you see these pictures there may be a lack of understanding. When you see the child that is so skinny and malnourished with the big belly because they don't have anything to eat, that's poverty. Or where people don't have clean water to drink and they have to drink from their bath water or dirty streams, that's poverty. There are a number of people that are still living like that today. Now there are plenty of mission organizations that are building water wells, setting up churches, setting up homes and feeding programs. They exist but it is not reaching every single person, not just yet. Kids going through the garbage cans to get scraps to eat or living on the streets is poverty. In India where they don't appreciate women, parents may kill the female children or allow them to starve to death. That's what poverty really looks like. So, if you don't have food, if you don't have water, you will not be able to live. Those are needs.

Imagine you are a child living in the streets of India. You are going through the garbage to find food. Your parents have left you. Now while you are digging through that garbage, you find a dollar. A dollar which you can use to go get something to eat. You find that dollar which is needed to sustain yourself or you will not be alive. You still have nothing to give to the Lord. Clearly this is not God's desire for His children.

Poverty says you are living in the land of lack. You don't have enough. Your sustenance for living is not amply supplied. You have nothing to give to the Lord. Anything that anyone gives to you is required to meet your basic needs. When they build a water well, they are meeting the water requirement. If they are having a feeding program, they are meeting the life sustaining food need. If they put up a new building for orphans, they are meeting the basic shelter necessity. A clothes closet or shoe providing program supplies the clothing requirement. Prosperity says you are living in either provision (all basic necessities are supplied) or you are living in abundance (a measure over necessities of which you can then give to the Lord).

There are three levels: poverty, provision and abundance. Poverty is living below your basic needs. You are living in lack. You don't have a sufficient supply. Enough is based on basic needs; food, clothes and shelter, not what you want.

PROVISION — Having your needs met.

Imagine another scenario, the children of Israel in the wilderness, their shoes never ran out and their clothes were the same. They still had clothes. It doesn't matter that they are 40 years old. Their basic needs were still met. God supplied what was required. He even rained down manna from heaven (Exodus 16).

Provision indicates that your needs are met. Let's look at Matthew chapter 6 where Jesus says, *"I say unto you take no thought for your life what you shall eat or what you shall drink nor for the body what you shall put on. Is not the life more than meat and the body more than rainment? Behold the fowls of the air, for they sow not neither do they reap nor gather into barns. Yet your heavenly Father feeds them. Are you not much better then they? Which of you by taking thought can add one cubit unto his stature? And why take ye thought for rainment. Consider the lilies of the field how they grow. They toil not neither do they spin and yet I say unto you that even Solomon in all his glory was not arrayed as one of these. Wherefore, if God so clothed the grass of the field which today is and tomorrow is cast into the oven shall he not much more cloth you? O ye of little faith. Therefore take not thought saying what shall we eat or what shall we drink or wherewith all shall we be clothed (for after all these things do the Gentiles seek – <u>those that are outside of the Kingdom, those that don't believe</u>) For your heavenly Father knoweth that you have need of these things. But seek ye first the Kingdom of God and His righteousness and all these things shall be* added unto you." *(Matthew 6:25-33, emphasis of clarity mine)*

In the 25th verse He says don't be overly concerned about your life clarified by basic needs. Your life is more than those needs. Considering the fact that God took care of the children of Israel as they wandered in the wilderness, He has a desire to take care of us too.

Verse 26 says, *"Behold the fowls of the air, for they sow not neither do they reap nor gather into barns. Yet your heavenly Father feeds them."* Provision says that you are going to be taken care of: that you are believing; you're recognizing; you're trusting; you're depending upon God to take care of your life sustaining requirements. You are in provision so you are kept. In our discussion on limitations, we will discover ignorance is one of the reasons. Another reason was that they didn't operate in or walk in the knowledge that they did know. It's important for us to comprehend that God's desire is to provide for us. If you don't believe that He will, you will try to go out in the world and make it on your own. So, if we know that is His desire, what will we do? We ask for it. *"Give us this day our daily bread (Matthew 6:11)."*

Every day Lord, we need to be able to eat. You said that you would cloth the birds of the field, you said you would take care of the sparrows so therefore we are asking you Father. You said we are worth more than a sparrow, we need food. We pray for daily bread. We need provision, so that's what we are requesting.

> **ABUNDANCE** — The measure above basic needs out of which you can give to the Lord.

Abundance is the measure above basic needs out of which you can give to the Lord. You have not just your required daily provisions but there is extra. In lack would equate to poverty. Then if your needs are met that is provision. But if you are above the basic needs, you're in abundance. You might think abundance is beyond your ability- silver and gold have I none (Acts 3:6) - and you reason, just give me the silver and gold. The significant monetary surplus is not what He refers to as abundance. Both abundance and provision are considered prosperity. God says we are supposed to have abundance (see John 10:10). That's why we discussed His will for us first.

"God says for my thoughts are not your thoughts. Neither are your ways my ways saith the Lord. For as the heavens are higher than the earth so are my ways higher than your ways and my thoughts higher than your thoughts. For as the rain comes down and the snow from heaven and returns not thither but water the earth and make it bring forth and bud that it may give seed to the sower and

bread to the eater so shall my word be that goes forth out of my mouth, it shall not return unto me void but it shall accomplish that which I please and it shall prosper thereto unto the thing which I sent it." *(Isaiah 55:8-11)*

God says, first of all we don't think alike. Your ways in which you normally operate are not My ways. We need to get on the same page with God. He has foresight in all of His planning and is thorough in His systems. He says just like the water that comes down from heaven we know it doesn't just mist and go back but it waters the grass (Isaiah 55:10). When it waters the grass the flowers bloom or a harvest sprouts or some plants grow. As it grows we also have seed. For example, we have apple trees. We eat apples and on the inside of the apple (core) are seeds. If you plant that seed, it will produce another apple tree. You will have seed for the sower, you will be able to plant it. You will have bread for food. In other words, since you already ate the apple, the seed allows you to have something else to plant. So not only do you have your basic needs met because you ate but you have something to give to the Lord, you have something to sow. That planting and sowing is above your life sustaining provision. Then Isaiah chapter 55 lets us know we have both. Bread for the eater is the provision, the food that we eat now. The seed for us to sow is the abundance. You take in what you need, you give what you can sow.

"And He said (he being Jesus) so is the kingdom of God as if a man should cast seed

into the ground and should sleep and rise night and day and the seed should spring and grow up he knoweth not how. For the earth bringeth forth fruit of herself. First the blade then the ear, after that the full corn in the ear. But when the fruit is brought forth immediately he puts it to the sickle because the harvest has come." (Mark 4:26-29)

The sower is going to eat what he planted at a later time when it is harvested. He doesn't know how it grows. When the seed is planted, we don't know how it becomes another apple tree. We don't know what is contained in the seed nor what causes it to sprout. But God says sow it and I will grow it.

After consideration of these three levels, where are you? How can you go from one level the to next? Do you see God's desire? Are you living in abundance?

> Abundant Living
> Bible Study
> Page 219

Chapter 4: Coming out of Poverty

We've talked about our definition of poverty as living in lack and being below our basic needs (insufficient supply). Poverty is a position in which we don't have anything that we can give to the Lord. We discussed the two levels of prosperity: you have provision meaning your basic needs are met; and then abundance which is a measure above basic needs where you can then turn around and give to the Lord.

Does anyone want to live in poverty? Of course, the answer is NO! In order to get to the level of provision we have to use our faith. Faith by definition is, our trust our reliance, our dependence upon God and giving credence to His word. We know that it is God's will that we have food, clothes and shelter. We can ask for the things that we need. If He takes care of the birds, if He clothes the lilies, He will do some of the same things for us; provide for our physical life needs. So how do we come out of poverty? We must do the work of faith, bind the enemy, dispatch angels and speak God's word. It's essential that we do the work of the hand. We have to receive of the promises through godly wisdom.

Work of Faith

> *"But without faith it is impossible to please Him (God); for he that cometh to God must first believe that He Is and that He is a rewarder of him that diligently seek him."* (Hebrews 11:6)

We need to start with knowing that God is going to reward us if we seek Him. We must have confidence in Him giving the weight of our concerns over to Him and fully expect Him to come through. What is the work of faith? In John's gospel chapter 6 verses 26 through 29, Jesus answers the question.

> *"Jesus answered them and said, Verily, verily, I say unto you, Ye seek me, not because ye saw the miracles, but because ye did eat of the loaves, and were filled. Labour not for the meat which perisheth, but for that meat which endureth unto everlasting life, which the Son of man shall give unto you: for him hath God the Father sealed. Then said they unto him, What shall we do, that we might work the works of God? Jesus answered and said unto them, <u>This is the work of God, that ye believe on him whom he hath sent.</u>"* (John 6:6-29, emphasis mine)

The work of faith is our believing on the Son of God, having full confidence in Jesus. Do you really believe that He lived? Do you believe the Father sent Him? Is He the Son of God born of a virgin delivering the message of salvation? Is He the representation of the Father in bodily form? Did He speak the words of God to the people? Are you confident that His crucifixion was an actual event? Do you trust that He resurrected from the dead? Are you seeking His face and not His hand? Are you following because you know He is the Son of God or are you only seeking to have your desires met?

In coming out of poverty the first step is to go into the level of provision. God promises to provide for His children. We first need to believe based on the work of faith. We declare that we are believing for provision because He promised. We declare that we are coming out of lack and want of poverty into provision because we stand on His word. We're putting our confidence and trust in the Word but what must we do to add feet to that belief? We pray. In Matthew 6:11 it says, **"Give us this day our daily bread".** That's part of the model prayer when the disciples asked Jesus to teach them to pray. And He said pray after this manner. He acknowledges who God is then in the midst of the prayer He says 'give us this day our daily bread'; not month of supply, not storehouse but daily. He prays that God provide, indispensable provision. When He rained manna from heaven, that was daily bread (Exodus 16). The children of Israel were being provided for were they not? Were not their basic needs met? They had food (manna), they had clothing (it never wore out), and they had a cloud by day and a pillar of fire by night. They were not in poverty, they were not in abundance they were in provision.

Actually, when the children of Israel came out of Egypt none of them were sick. And none of them got sick. Now they may have died because of a serpent bite because they did something wrong, declaring 'oh we have sinned'. (Numbers 21:6-7) That occurred but they didn't come out of Egypt with sicknesses. That was not God's design for them. So, if we are going to come out of poverty, living in lack below basic needs, we have to work the work of faith, believing in the Son of God. Secondarily we're going to ask Him to give us this indispensable provision, our daily bread.

Binding the Enemy

Another thing we need to do to come out of poverty is bind the enemy. In other words, we are going to restrain the thief, the devourer, our opposer. In John 10:10 Jesus says **'but the thief comes only but to steal kill and destroy but I am come that you might have life and have it more abundantly'**. The thief's desire is to take from you what you have. To steal from you so that you don't enjoy what has been provided. A thief (*kleptēs*) steals by fraud and in secret. It metaphorically relates to false teachers or deceivers who steal men away from the truth. Who is the thief in your life? What's taking you from your abundance? Where is it going?

Many promises especially for provision have been given to us. The enemy's desire is for us to not walk in them and he must be prevented from accomplishing his mission. If Jesus came for us to have this abundant life we definitely should not be in poverty. Knowing Him, trusting Him, relying upon Him, and asking Him to give us daily bread is our start. In Matthew 12:28-29. Jesus said, *'If I cast out devils by the spirit of God then the Kingdom of God has come unto you. Or else how can one enter into a strong man's house and spoil his goods except he first bind the strong man and then he will spoil his house'*. You can't take from somebody who is protecting their house. If they have it already secured and on lock down you can't get in to get their possessions. So, if the enemy is trying to come and steal from you, you have to restrain him so that he cannot enter and pilfer what belongs to you. The word bind means to restrain. It has the connotation of you preventing the ability to loot.

Jesus gives us authority to bind and loose in Matthew 18:18-20. *"Verily I say unto you, Whatsoever ye shall bind on earth shall be bound in heaven: and whatsoever ye shall loose on earth shall be loosed in heaven. Again I say unto you, That if two of you shall agree on earth as touching any thing that they shall ask, it shall be done for them of my Father which is in heaven. For where two or three are gathered together in my name, there am I in the midst of them."* He reiterates that authority in Matthew 16:19. Jesus said, *'I will give unto thee the keys of the kingdom of heaven and whatsoever you bind on earth will be bound in heaven and whatsoever you loose on earth will be loosed in heaven'*. In other words, whatever you restrain here on earth is going to be restrained in heaven, whatever you free or let loose will be loosed also in heaven. Jesus died and gave us the keys to do this and we ought to use it, it's one of our tools. It is part of our work of faith, Why? Because as we work faith, we are trusting, relying, depending upon the Word and using the Word we declare God's promises and protection. He said He's given us these keys that we can use. The keys represent the authority or power. He's given us the authority to restrain the hand of the enemy and to free promises. If you don't believe you have the power to stand against the attacks of the enemy you won't. But if you believe that you can and you use the authority adequately according to what His word says and you believe you're going to receive, that's what you get. So, we are going to bind the enemy. Let's undergird more with Matthew 18. Part of what we do in binding the enemy is that we are obedient to God's word so we don't allow him a foothold to enter. We can go back to Haggai where God says your clothes are going to be as if you have pockets with holes in them because you are spending them on yourself and it's running out (Haggai 1:6). The prophet Malachi says of God, **"I will open up the windows of heaven and pour you out a blessing you don't have room enough to receive And I will rebuke the devourer for your sakes, and he shall not destroy the fruits of your ground; neither shall your vine cast her fruit before the time in the field, saith the LORD of hosts." (Malachi 3:10-11)** That doesn't happen normally. That promise is fulfilled when you are in covenant relationship (more on this topic later in the book). God says not only will He open up the windows of heaven and bless you abundantly but He will rebuke the one whose desire is to destroy all that you have, if you keep covenant. Rebuking the devourer is equivalent to restraining or binding the enemy. He can't consume your crops. He can't put holes in your pockets thereby stealing your money. And he can't take from you and destroy your income source.

Often God will send a test to see if you will be obedient. God's provision may come in different ways. He may have somebody bring it to your doorstep or allow you to purchase children's shoes inexpensively at a garage sale. It doesn't matter how it happens, it is God providing for you. Recognize the sustaining ability God makes for you regardless of the circumstances. He's our provider, sustainer, and maintainer!

Looking at the poverty side and how to come out, Why do we have different ministries that go in to meet the basic needs? The people don't have water, so ministries build a water well. They put up a church right next to the well so that their physical needs and their spiritual needs can be met. Then the Pastor becomes the number one person that everybody wants to know. The community comes, they go to service, they hear about Jesus and they get the water. They not only get the water for their physical bodies but they get the living water for their souls. Why? Because one of the things we said you have to do to come out of poverty is to do the work of faith. They introduce the community to Jesus and what He has already done for them so they then ask for and trust Him for daily provision.

They begin by helping them along the way but they will not always be the one providing for them. They make sure they point them to the ultimate supplier. The blinded eyes are now open and the enemy oppressing them can no longer run rampant.

Dispatch Ministering Angels

We can also dispatch ministering angels according to Matthew 4:11. Let's start with the fact that angels do come and minister to us. Matthew 4:10 records, Jesus said get thee hence Satan. Jesus is in the wilderness tempted of Satan and finally has enough. **"Thou shall worship the Lord your God and him only shall you serve."** *(Matthew 4:10)* Verse 11 records, then the devil leaves Him and behold angels came and ministered unto him. Angels came and attended to Jesus. He didn't even have to call them but they came. Hebrews 1:13 states, **"But to which of the angels said he at any time sit on my right hand until I make thy enemies thy footstool."** We know God told Jesus to sit on his right hand. Angels were never given that privilege and authority. Verse 14 states, **"Are they not all ministering spirits sent forth for them to minister to them who are to be heirs of salvation."** Angels are ministering spirits sent forth to minister, to assist. The question is who are they assisting? According to the Word, they are assisting the heirs of salvation. Who then are the heirs of salvation? We are. Angels have a purpose. Their purpose is to attend to us, the heirs of salvation, one who has an inheritance. Psalm 91:11 tells us that God is going to give His angels charge over us to keep us in all our ways. Angels according to Scripture come and assist us and they are commissioned to keep us as we keep going. Psalm 103:20 says, *"Bless the Lord ye his angels that excel in strength that do his commandments hearkening unto the voice of his word."* If you have the word of God in your mouth and you're asking those things to be done, angels are listening with the intent to perform those commands. So, when you say, "Father you said that you would send your angels to take charge over me that they are going to keep me, that they will be stationed round about me. God, I need your protection, Lord I need your angels to minister to me"; they obey. If that's in His word and it is a promise in His word, then when you speak that request they are standing ready to obey that command. If you utter His word then you are dispatching them. Angels are standing ready at attention. They don't have to wait for anything. They know God's word, and they follow God's word, period. If you allow the Word to come out of your mouth, angels will obey that Word. Angels are created beings, they are not human. The Bible says they look on us in awe and wonder about salvation (1 Peter 1:12). They don't understand how God's mercy and His grace has been expressed upon us and that we're heirs of salvation because they are not. Angels are not like us in that sometimes we don't obey God's word. We have the ability when we speak God's word that the angels will run to assist and to accomplish what God promised. What we are doing is speaking back to God His very word. We remind God what He promised in His word and we are asking that it be done. We have so much more ability and authority than we utilize. The problem is we don't recognize what we have nor use our authority. God said He will do exceeding abundantly above all that we could hope, ask or think according to the power that works in us (Ephesians 3:20). Well, what power is that? The Holy Spirit resides in us. Jesus died and now we've got the keys to the Kingdom. He gave us authority to bind and to loose and it will happen based on our confidence. He said if you need something and it's in the Word, and you speak the Word the angels are going to come running (or flying) to get it done. We don't realize the authority and power that we have been given.

In Matthew 18:10, Jesus said, *"Take heed that you despise not one of these little ones for I say unto you that in heaven their angels always do behold the face of my father which is in heaven."* Children have their own angels. We have angels assigned to us as well. They are clothed in strength (Psalm 103) they are powerful, they are big, they are mighty, they can do so much more but what are they going to do? His word. They are obedient to God's word. You speak His word, they go into action. They are waiting on you. They are waiting to be commissioned to go and do something but when we keep it inside they remain still. Open your mouth!

Divine Summons
(according to the word of God)

"For the promise, that he should be the heir of the world, was not to Abraham, or to his seed, through the law, but through the righteousness of faith (our trust, our reliance, our dependence on God). *For if they which are of the law be heirs, faith is made void* (of none effect), *and the promise made of none effect: Because the law worketh wrath* (anger): *for where no law is, there is no transgression. Therefore it is of faith, that it might be by grace; to the end the promise might be sure to all the seed; not to that only which is of the law, but to that also which is of the faith of Abraham; who is the father of us all, (As it is written, I have made thee a father of many nations,) before him whom he believed,* <u>*even God, who quickeneth the dead, and calleth those things which be not as though they were.*</u> *Who against hope believed in hope, that he might become the father of many nations, according to that which was spoken, So shall thy seed be. And being not weak in faith, he considered not his own body now dead, when he was about an hundred years old, neither yet the deadness of Sara's womb: He staggered not at the promise of God through unbelief; but was strong in faith, giving glory to God; And being fully persuaded that, what he had promised, he*

was able also to perform. And therefore it was imputed to him for righteousness. Now it was not written for his sake alone, that it was imputed to him; But for us also, to whom it shall be imputed, if we believe on him that raised up Jesus our Lord from the dead; Who was delivered for our offences, and was raised again for our justification." (Romans 4:13-25, clarification and emphasis mine)

If we didn't have the speed limit sign posted indicating that the limit is 25 mph then regardless of how fast we drive we would not receive a ticket. You would not be breaking the law because if there is no law you cannot transgress it. Transgress by definition is to infringe or go beyond the bounds of (a moral principle or other established standard or behavior): to violate a command or law; sin. Verse 16 states, **"Therefore it is of faith that it might be by grace to the end that the promise might be sure to all the seed."** The seed would include every generation; the offspring that came from Abraham. **"Not to those only of the law but to those also that is of faith"** (verse 16b). Those who by grace are saved through faith in God would be included. Not necessarily born from Abraham's loin but Abraham's heirs. Gentiles are then grafted in making Abraham the father of us all. We would be included in the privileges of the promise. Verse 17 is parenthetical – **"for I have made thee a father of many nations. Before whom he believed, even God, who quickeneth the dead and calls those things that be not as though they were."** As a note here, we recognize that God is the one that called those things into being that previously did not exist. *"Who against hope believed in hope that he might become the father of many nations."* (vs 18) God is the one that called those things that were not yet as though they had already occurred. You may recall that when Abraham was well up in years and his wife Sarah was barren that God spoke that they would have a son. That seemed to be an impossible situation yet God spoke it into existence. So now if we get on the same page with God and say those things that God says, then yes, we can give that divine summons but He (God) is really the one summoning. We are just repeating His word. Some have said that we should command His hand, i.e. command God to do what we want. But God is not our cosmic bellhop. He is not our Santa Claus in the sky. We don't tell God what to do. His purpose is not to meet our every whim so that's not what we are doing.

Remember the *'Bruce Almighty'* movie when Jim Carrey, playing God, decided to grant all the prayers with a 'yes'. Everything was topsy-turvy. We don't just rub a lamp and wha-la, your wish is my command. With this understanding it cuts out all the name it and claim it propaganda. So, then the work of faith is important; we believe in God's word and act upon it dispatching angels as needed but saying what God already promised.

Work of the Hand

"And we have confidence in the Lord concerning you, that you are doing and will continue to do the things which we suggest and with which we charge you. May the Lord direct your hearts into [realizing and showing] the love of God and into the steadfastness and patience of Christ and in waiting for His return. Now we charge you, brethren, in the name and on the authority of our Lord Jesus Christ (the Messiah) that you withdraw and keep away from every brother (fellow believer) who is slack in the performance of duty and is disorderly, living as a shirker and not walking in accord with the traditions and instructions that you have received from us. For you yourselves know how it is necessary to imitate our example, for we were not disorderly or shirking of duty when we were with you [we were not idle]. Nor did we eat anyone's bread without paying for it, but with toil and struggle we worked night and day, that we might not be a burden or impose on any of you [for our support]. [It was] not because we do not have a right [to such support], but [we wished] to make ourselves an example for you to follow. For while we were yet with you, we gave you this rule and charge: If anyone will not work, neither let him eat. Indeed, we hear that some among you are disorderly [that they are

passing their lives in idleness, neglectful of duty], being busy with other people's affairs instead of their own and doing no work. Now we charge and exhort such persons [as ministers of Him exhorting those] in the Lord Jesus Christ (the Messiah) that they work in quietness and earn their own food and necessities." (2 Thessalonians 3:4-12, AMP)

There is an admonition or encouragement that we need to work. It is very clear from the amplified version that we should not sit idle. A man that doesn't work shouldn't expect others to handle their neglect. This passage makes it clear that shirking responsibility is not the Biblical standard. We should take note of those that fall into these categories and avoid the same trap.

There is also a warning of laziness in Proverbs 6: 6-11, *"Go to the ant you sluggard, consider her ways and be wise. Which having no guide or overseer or ruler provideth her meat in the summer and gathers her food in the harvest. How long will thy sleep o sluggard? When will thy arise out of thy sleep? Yet a little sleep, a little slumber, a little folding of the hands to sleep. So shall thy poverty come as one that traveleth and thy want as an armed man."* God's word reminds us that if we keep being lazy there will be an undesired result. The ant is not lazy. The ant gets up and gathers his food so that he can eat later on. God tells us to not be lazy. If you sleep, folding your hands, watching your favorite show (soap operas, sports events, etc.), sitting in front of the tv doing absolutely nothing and you are not working but you are waiting on a check to come in every month, eventually it is going to run out. He says surely poverty is going to come upon you.

Not only do we have to work faith but we have to put in the effort to get something accomplished. We need to add feet to our faith. The third category to come out of poverty is receiving of the promise through godly wisdom.

Godly Wisdom

If God knows He can trust you, He will give you what you need. If we are going to receive the promise through godly wisdom we must have our motives right. Wisdom is being skillful in the things and the word of God. We need to be proficient in it, we need to know it, we need to trust it. And we need to have a right motive regarding the Word. It means that you are not giving so that you can get. But you have to recognize God's promises are yes and amen, they are true. We need to approach God appropriately with the right attitude. Let's look at Solomon's example of wisdom in 1 Kings 3: 5-14, *"In Gibeon the Lord appeared to Solomon by night, and God said ask what I should give thee, Solomon said thou has shown unto my father David great mercy according as he has walked before thee in truth and in righteousness and in uprightness of heart with thee and thou has kept for him this great kindness that thou has given him a son to sit on the throne as it is this day. And now*

O Lord, my God thou has made thy servant king instead of David my father, and I am but a little child, I know not how to go out or to come in, and thy servant is in the midst of thy people a great people, that cannot be numbered nor counted for the multitude. Give therefore thy servant an understanding heart to judge thy people that I may discern between good and bad for who is able to judge this thy so great a people."

Solomon was wise. Paraphrasing what he said to God, "You put me on the throne, you did what you said you were going to do for my father David. You put me as heir to be the next King and I am but a little child. Now my dad walked before you like he was supposed to, upright. So, if you are asking me what I should ask you, help me to judge right. Give me understanding so that I can judge appropriately. This is a great people you have. These are your chosen people and I recognize it but I can't do it without you, I just need understanding, I need wisdom."

It goes on to say, it pleased God in verse 10, **"And the speech pleased the Lord, that Solomon had asked this thing and God said unto him because though has asked this thing and has not asked for thyself long life** (he wasn't being selfish), **neither has though asked riches for thyself, nor has asked the life of thy enemies but has asked for understanding judgment behold I have done according to thy words. Lo, I have given thee a wise and an understanding heart so that there was none like** *thee before thee neither after thee nor any arise unto thee (commentary mine)."* God responds to Solomon remarking that he is going to be in a class by himself when it comes to his request. God indicated that He is giving him the wisdom and a heart like nobody else ever had because he asked. No one will have that heart after him either.

Verse 13 continues, *"and I have also given thee that which thou has not asked for".* Because Solomon asked with the unselfish motivation God says I'm going to give you extra – exceeding abundantly. How much more? So much more! What you haven't asked for God says, I'm going to give you, *"riches and the honor so that there shall not be any among the Kings like unto thee all thy days. And if thy will walk in my ways to keep my statutes and my commandments that thy father David did and will walk in my ways all of your days".* Solomon didn't ask selfishly but he received in excess of his request for wisdom. Solomon's example was receiving the promise through godly wisdom.

> *"Happy is the man that findeth wisdom, and the man that getteth understanding. For the merchandise of it is better than the merchandise of silver, and the gain thereof than fine gold. She is more precious than rubies: and all the things thou canst desire are not to be compared unto her. Length of days is in her right hand; and in her left hand riches and honour. Her ways are ways of*

pleasantness, and all her paths are peace. She is a tree of life to them that lay hold upon her: and happy is every one that retaineth her. The LORD by wisdom hath founded the earth; by understanding hath he established the heavens. By his knowledge the depths are broken up, and the clouds drop down the dew." (Proverbs 3:13-20)

Notice that with the wisdom came a multitude of benefits. The wealth and respect and longevity were added. These bring freedom from worry of meeting needs, a good report and increased days to enjoy the blessings. If you have wisdom you have peace because you will also know how to answer appropriately.

"**Lay not up for yourselves treasures on earth where moth and rust doth corrupt and where thieves break through and steal. But lay up for yourselves treasures in heaven where moth and rust doth not corrupt and thieves do not break through and steal. For where your treasure is there will your heart be also. The light of the body is the eye and therefore if thy eye be single thy whole body will be full of light. But if thy eye be evil thy whole body shall be full of darkness therefore if thy light that is in thee be full of darkness, how great is that darkness. No man can serve two masters for he will love the one and hate the other or he will hold to the one and despise** the other. You can not serve both God and mammon. Therefore I say take no thought..." (Matthew 6:19-34)

Your treasure, the things that you value the most, should not be the things you store on earth because they get old, they rust, and it will be junk soon. But the things that you store up in heaven will not corrode or become useless. The toys, cars, precious gems, and even cash that so many consider important here on earth have no value or purpose in heaven. The Bible even identifies that you can't take it with you (1 Timothy 6:7). So, make sure your treasure is above. That would be the wise thing to do.

As we continue with godly wisdom we see our wisdom is in Christ. In 1 Corinthians 1:26-31, AMP (emphasis mine) it says, *"For [simply] consider your own call, brethren, not many [of you were considered to be] wise according to human estimates and standards, not many influential and powerful, not many of high and noble birth. [No] for God selected (deliberately chose) what in the world is foolish to put the wise to shame, and what the world calls weak to put the strong to shame. And God also selected (deliberately chose) what in the world is lowborn and insignificant and branded and treated with contempt, even the things that are nothing, that He might depose and bring to nothing the things that are. So that no mortal man should [have pretense for glorying and] boast in the presence of God. <u>But it is from Him that you have your life in</u>*

Christ Jesus, Whom God made our Wisdom from God, [revealed to us a knowledge of the divine plan of salvation previously hidden, manifesting itself as] our Righteousness [thus making us upright and putting us in right standing with God], and our Consecration [making us pure and holy], and our Redemption [providing our ransom from eternal penalty for sin]. So then, as it is written, Let him who boasts and proudly rejoices and glories, boast and proudly rejoice and glory in the Lord." Based on what Christ has done, God shows His wisdom by His righteousness, sanctification and His redemption which we have all in Christ. All the credit then should be shifted to Him. Though we carry out the actions we recognize that our strength and abilities come from Him. All the acclaim goes to God because He is worthy of the praise.

Add to that Scripture, Colossians 2:1-3 (emphasis mine), *"For I would that you knew what great conflict I have for you and for them at Laodicia, and for as many as have not seen my face in the flesh that their hearts might be comforted being knit together in love and unto all riches of the full assurance of understanding and to the acknowledgement of the mystery of God and of the Father and of Christ in whom are hid all the treasures of wisdom and knowledge"*. All the wealth of skill in the affairs of life and intelligence and comprehension are hidden in God. Think about the mystery, Christ came and died that while we were yet sinners He sacrificed because He wanted to redeem us

– righteousness, sanctification and redemption. He attributed to our account His right standing with God because of His sinless life. He works with us to conform us to His image. And through His death He bought us back paying the price for our freedom. It is foolishness to mere mortal man, it doesn't make any sense. The treasure is in what He has already done. Christ gave His life for us so that He could ransom us from the penalty of sin which is death. He, Christ, was and is righteous, blameless before God. He didn't owe a debt for sin but He took on our debt. And then He goes on to say now you go and do likewise; Do good to those who despitefully use and abuse you (Matthew 5:44). It doesn't matter that you were betrayed, denied or sold out, it doesn't matter Jesus says, take comfort, so did they do to the prophets before you. In other words, you are in good company.

So that's how we come out of poverty: the work of faith; the work of the hand; and receiving the promises through Godly wisdom. Are you ready to go on to provision?

> **Coming out of Poverty Bible Study Page 221**

Chapter 5: Going onto Abundance

Once we have come out of poverty we are prosperous at the provision level. Our ultimate aim is the land of plenty. In order to get to abundance, we must establish in our hearts if God promised it in His covenant. Did He promise prosperity? The word prosperity in the King James version and other translations does not always mean wealth and riches; it does not always have to do with just money.

Let's look at a few passages:

3 John 2, *"Beloved I wish above all things that you prosper and be in good health even as your soul prospers"*. The word prosper here is *euodoo* {yoo-od-o-o} meaning to grant a prosperous and an expeditious journey; in other words, to be successful. In the NIV version the same passage reads, *"Dear friend, I pray that you may enjoy good health and that all may go well with you, even as your soul is getting along well."* The desire is that we are successful and have a prosperous life. This life would include health as our soul (mind, will, and emotions) are enlightened. There

is a correlation between our understanding or spiritual life and our success.

Joshua 1:7-8 in the Amplified Bible says, *"Only you be strong and very courageous, that you may do according to all the law which Moses My servant commanded you. Turn not from it to the right hand or to the left, that you may prosper wherever you go. This Book of the Law shall not depart out of your mouth, but you shall meditate on it day and night, that you may observe and do according to all that is written in it. For then you shall make your way prosperous, and then you shall deal wisely and have good success."* Prosperous here deals with acting or doing wisely. It is the Hebrew word *sakal* {saw-kal} meaning to be prudent, circumspect, wisely understand, act prudently, to act circumspectly, to act wisely. The encouragement then is as we follow the Word we will make wise decisions and have a fruitful outcome.

Psalm 35:27, *"Let them shout for joy, and be glad, that favour my righteous cause: yea, let them say continually, Let the LORD be magnified, which hath pleasure in the prosperity of his servant."* Here prosperity is the Hebrew word *shalom* {shaw-lome} meaning peace or perfect peace and well-being. Completeness soundness and welfare is also in the definition. In the NIV version it reads, *"May those who delight in my vindication shout for joy and gladness; may they always say, 'The LORD be exalted, who delights in the well-being of his *servant.'"* This translation shows the indication of welfare as a desired goal of our Father.

Psalm 1:1-3, AMP, *"**Blessed (HAPPY, fortunate, prosperous, and enviable) is the man who walks and lives not in the counsel of the ungodly [following their advice, their plans and purposes], nor stands [submissive and inactive] in the path where sinners walk, nor sits down [to relax and rest] where the scornful [and the mockers] gather. But his delight and desire are in the law of the Lord, and on His law (the precepts, the instructions, the teachings of God) he habitually meditates (ponders and studies) by day and by night. And he shall be like a tree firmly planted [and tended] by the streams of water, ready to bring forth its fruit in its season; its leaf also shall not fade or wither; and everything he does shall prosper [and come to maturity].*" Prosperity here is the Hebrew word *tsalach* {tsaw-lakh}. The definition is to push forward; to come to maturity; to advance; to make progress; to be profitable; to succeed. Jeremiah 17:7-8 takes the same symbolism of a tree being planted and continuing to grow regardless of circumstances. It helps add to our understanding of this prosperous maturing. *"**[Most] blessed is the man who believes in, trusts in, and relies on the Lord, and whose hope and confidence the Lord is. For he shall be like a tree planted by the waters that spreads out its roots by the river; and it shall not see and fear when heat comes; but its leaf shall be green. It shall not be anxious and full of care in the year of drought, nor shall it cease yielding fruit.*"

(Jeremiah 17:7-8). The one trusting in the Lord shall spread out their roots and persevere through dry times and continue to mature.

Now of the four passages we expounded on, none refer to money. Prosperity as we have covered means to have a good journey; to act wisely; to have peace; and to push forward. There are however, instances where Scripture actually promises financial or material goods and wealth.

Psalm 112:1-3 AMP, *"PRAISE THE Lord! (Hallelujah!) Blessed (happy, fortunate, to be envied) is the man who fears (reveres and worships) the Lord, who delights greatly in His commandments. His [spiritual] offspring shall be mighty upon earth; the generation of the upright shall be blessed. Prosperity and welfare are in his house, and his righteousness endures forever."*

Proverbs 10:22 *"The blessing of the LORD, it maketh rich, and he addeth no sorrow with it."* In the NIV version it reads, *"The blessing of the LORD brings wealth, and he adds no trouble to it."*

Proverbs 22:4 *"By humility and the fear of the LORD are riches, and honour, and life."*

2 Corinthians 8:9 *"For ye know the grace of our Lord Jesus Christ, that, though he was rich* (4145), *yet for your sakes he became poor, that ye through his poverty might be rich* (4147).*"*

> **RICH**
> 4145 πλούσιος [*plousios /ploo·see·os/*] 1 wealthy, abounding in material resources. 2 metaph. abounding, abundantly supplied. 2a abounding (rich) in Christian virtues and eternal possessions.
> 4147 πλουτέω [*plouteo /ploo·teh·o/*] 1 to be rich, to have abundance. 1a of outward possessions. 2 metaph. to be richly supplied. 2a is affluent in resources so that he can give blessings of salvation to all.
> Strong, J. (1995). <u>Enhanced Strong's Lexicon.</u> <u>Woodside Bible Fellowship.</u>

2 Corinthians 9:8-11 **"And God is able to make all grace abound toward you; that ye, always having all sufficiency in all things, may abound to every good work: (As it is written, He hath dispersed abroad; he hath given to the poor: his righteousness remaineth for ever. Now he that ministereth seed to the sower both minister bread for your food, and multiply your seed sown, and increase the fruits of your righteousness;) Being enriched in every thing to all bountifulness, which causeth through us thanksgiving to God."**

All of these passages refer to actual riches and wealth or money. As we look back on Isaiah 55 previously examined, we see that the word *prosperity* is not just money but God does promise riches and wealth; honor; a good journey; acting wisely; peace; and maturity. Therefore, when we look at the three levels that we have, we show poverty, provision as well as abundance.

There are requirements to move from one level to the next. Coming out of poverty which is our lowest level we need the work of faith; we need to work with our hands (we can't be lazy, we can't be idle); and receive the promises through godly wisdom. We have to also believe that the promises of God are available to us and that we will then stand on the promises. If you work the Word then the Word will work for you! The provision level assumes a desire to go on into abundance requiring we recognize what provision is and that God promises even more. For example, we want peace which is a part of prosperity, if you have peace as you live in this chaotic world you have a lot. If you have the riches and the honor you have even more. If you know how to act wisely having a good journey being successful you are well-off. If you are obeying His word, not turning to the left nor to the right, you are also successful. It's not only that you have money in your pocket and can spend it, it's a multitude of benefits. Prosperity encompasses more than just riches and honor.

"But now hath he obtained a more excellent ministry, by how much also he is the mediator of a better covenant, which was established upon better promises." (Hebrews 8:6)

God promised a lot to Abraham in the Old Testament. He promised it not only to him but to his seed (his heirs). The author of Hebrews goes back through all the promises in the Old Testament and reminds us what God has promised to His Chosen People, Israel.

He turns around and says now that old covenant was a great covenant (Old Testament). There are an abundance of promises recorded but when Jesus came He gave us a better covenant, not only do you have the old but you have the new. Therefore, we have a better covenant now that we are New Testament believers. The package deal adds new promises to the existing ones. Jesus died to give us both. We call Him faithful; it says He's faithful in the Old Testament. We say that He can do miracles; He did miracles in the Old Testament and the New Testament. He is Jehovah-Jireh our provider; that's Old Testament. Abraham and Sarah having a child; Old Testament miracle. As God was with Moses he declared, *"Moses my servant is dead" (Joshua 1:2)* and did the same things for Joshua. God said to David He would make sure there would be a king that sits on the throne forever after his line. Solomon came after David and asked only for wisdom and God gave him that and then some.

Did not David say, *"I was young and now I'm old and I've never seen the righteous forsaken nor his seed begging bread." (Psalm 37:25) "I would have fainted if I did not think I would see the goodness of God in the land of the living." (Psalm 27:13)* All of that is in the Old Testament. We want the angels to minister to us, to take charge over us in all of our ways (Psalm 91:11) and then Jesus jumps on board and he says based on that faith not only do you have life but you have eternal life (John 10:10).

When God gave us in the book that pertains to life and godliness (The Bible) we received great and precious promises; a better covenant. Better *krite-tohn* in the Greek from Strong's *#2904 krato*s speaks of being stronger, more nobler, the best. The word *kratos* in the Greek, meaning vigor. Other words used to translate this word would be dominion, might, power and strength. It gives you the impressive expression of having bigger or having dominion, might, power and strength. Therefore, when we say it's a better covenant, it's a stronger covenant, it is the best covenant you could ever have!

Let's look at some additional Scriptural references:

> Jeremiah 31:31-34 (emphasis mine) *"Behold, the days come, saith the LORD, that I will make a <u>new covenant</u> with the house of Israel, and with the house of Judah: Not according to the covenant that I made with their fathers in the day that I took them by the hand to bring them out of the land of Egypt; which my covenant they brake, although I was an husband unto them, saith the LORD: But this shall be the covenant that I will make with the house of Israel; After those days, saith the LORD, <u>I will put my law in their inward parts, and write it in their hearts; and will be their God, and they shall be my people.</u>"*

Hebrews 9:15 (emphasis mine) *"And for this cause he is the mediator of the <u>new testament</u>, that by means of death, for the redemption of the transgressions that were under the first testament, they which are called might receive <u>the promise of eternal inheritance.</u>"*

Hebrews 12:24 (emphasis mine) *"And to Jesus the mediator of the <u>new covenant</u>, and to the blood of sprinkling, that speaketh <u>better things</u> than that of Abel."*

We have a better covenant and should be thankful that we are on this side of the covenant than on the Old Testament side. Not that the promises in the Old Testament are to be overlooked. God kept them, protected them, provided for them, and we have His names as a record to prove it; yet there was more to come. God has done so much for us, so richly blessed us, and He continues to back all those promises. Though we know what they are we need to believe that they are available for us today. Abundance can be yours. Do you know the Scriptural ways to achieve abundance?

> Going onto Abundance Bible Study Page 223

Chapter 6: Scriptural Ways to Achieve Abundance

FAVOR
- Preference for one person, group, etc. over another
- Something done or granted out of good will, rather than for justice or for remuneration
- The state of being approved or held in regard
- Excessive kindness or unfair partiality; preferential treatment
- To prefer; treat with partiality

Favor does come by way of our faith in God. When we trust – Totally surrender. Rest from fleshly labor. Understand God is working. Seek His face. Thank Him in advance. – God can grant us extra kindnesses. We all like favor, it sounds good and it makes us realize we have preferential treatment. In order to walk in treatment of partiality, we have to exercise faith in the principle of favor. Throughout history God has shown good will and approval to many people. Let's look at several examples:

> *"And Abel, he also brought of the firstlings of his flock and of the fat thereof. And the LORD had respect unto Abel and to his offering:" (Genesis 4:4)*

God gave favor to Abel; He honored his offering because he gave of his best. The approval given was because he saw Abel's heart. He wasn't giving God just something that he had. He gave the best that he had.

> *"And the LORD said, My spirit shall not always strive with man, for that he also is flesh: yet his days shall be an hundred and twenty years. There were giants in the earth in those days; and also after that, when the sons of God came in unto the daughters of men, and they bare children to them, the same became mighty men which were of old, men of renown. And GOD saw that the wickedness of man was great in the earth, and that every imagination of the thoughts of his heart was only evil continually. And it repented the LORD that he had made man on the earth, and it grieved him at his heart. And the LORD said, I will destroy man whom I have created from the face of the earth; both man, and beast, and the creeping thing, and*

the fowls of the air; for it repenteth me that I have made them. But Noah found grace in the eyes of the LORD." (Genesis 6:3-8)

We know everything on earth was going to be destroyed however Noah and his family were saved (rescued). They were hand chosen by God and shown preferential treatment.

There are several other men and women of favor In the Bible. They include Joseph, Daniel, Esther, David, Solomon, Samuel, Abraham, Israel and Jacob to name a few. Let's look at a couple (Joseph and Daniel and save the rest for Bible Study):

Joseph was a man that received favor; we read the story of Joseph in Genesis 37-47. He received this preferential treatment in a foreign land. His brothers plotted to kill him but they ended up selling him into slavery. He winds up in Potiphar's house falsely accused by Potiphar's wife. He then goes to prison. You are probably thinking, how is this favor? When you research the punishment, you realize he should have received the death penalty; he was supposed to die. That was the law. Even if he was falsely accused the death penalty was to be imposed. He received excessive kindness because he was required only to go to prison. He was then forgotten for the kindness he showed to others and was left in prison. Joseph was an interpreter of dreams. Joseph told the chief butler to remember him when he got out; and he didn't remember immediately. Some time down the road it was remembered that he interpreted accurately his dream when one was sought to interpret the dream of Pharaoh. Joseph was blessed by God to interpret Pharaoh's dream. Joseph was given the position of being second-in-command in Egypt; that's favor. If you want to look at the preparation of Joseph we must go to Psalm 105:15-21: *"Saying, Touch not mine anointed, and do my prophets no harm."* As a side note, when he's talking about the anointed ones, he is speaking of Israel. Verse 16, *"moreover he called for famine upon the land: he brake the whole staff of bread. He sent a man before them, even Joseph, who was sold for a servant: Whose feet they hurt with fetters: he was laid in iron: Until the time that his word came: the word of the LORD tried him. The king sent and loosed him; even the ruler of the people, and let him go free. He made him lord of his house, and ruler of all his substance."*

Based on the passage we recognize Joseph was destined to be in prison. He was tried; this particular trying was ordained to fuse him. Intended to melt and mold him so that he trusted and depended on nobody but God. Can you imagine being Joseph? All he could do was trust God. God was the one giving him the dreams, and allowing him to interpret the dreams. God was directing his steps all the way. Later he meets his brothers and declares what they meant for evil, God meant for good. The word that God gave him about his destiny took a while to come to pass; remember he was the dreamer. His brothers didn't like the thought of bowing down to Joseph and may have said so with disdain. The dream also showed the parents were bowing down to Joseph too.

The word God gave to Joseph about his destiny did not come true until he was molded. There was a time and there was a season before it came to fruition. These things occurred in order that he would be prepared to do all that was necessary.

Joseph received favor not only from God but also with man.

"And Joseph was brought down to Egypt; and Potiphar, an officer of Pharaoh, captain of the guard, an Egyptian, bought him of the hands of the Ishmaelites, which had brought him down thither." (Genesis 39:1)

"And his master saw that the LORD was with him, and that the LORD made all that he did to prosper in his hand. And Joseph found grace in his sight, and he served him: and he made him overseer over his house, and all that he had he put into his hand. And it came to pass from the time that he had made him overseer in his house, and over all that he had, that the LORD blessed the Egyptian's house for Joseph's sake; and the blessing of the LORD was upon all that he had in the house, and in the field. And he left all that he had in Joseph's hand; and he knew not ought he had, save the bread which he did eat. And

Joseph was a goodly person, and well favoured." (Genesis 39:3-6)

Joseph was well favored. Instead of being jealous when God is blessing others, just stand in their wake. Instead of getting upset since you are content – auto-sufficient in what Christ is blessing you with - be happy that favor is still evident. Don't be covetous; instead of desiring what Joseph had, do like the governor and let him handle your fortune.

Another way to be favored is to not accept the past as a rule for the future. Just because you did not walk in favor in the past; just because you messed up in the past is not an indication of your lack of favor for future experiences. You are learning now and we are going to take the word and let the word work for us.

Let's now turn our attention to Daniel:

"In the third year of the reign of Jehoiakim king of Judah came Nebuchadnezzar king of Babylon unto Jerusalem, and besieged it." (Daniel 1:1)

Daniel's name means 'God is my judge'. Daniel and his friends, the three Hebrew boys, were given names to glorify God. Nebuchadnezzar changed Daniel's name to Belteshazzar meaning 'Baal shall protect'. His friends were also given pagan names which would remove and replace who they were supposed to be worshipping. Hananiah means 'God is gracious'. His name was changed to Shadrach meaning 'inspiration of the Sun'; identifying the Sun god. Mishael meaning 'God who is without equal'. His name was changed to Meshach meaning 'belonging to Acku'. Acku is another god. Azariah's name means 'the Lord is my helper'. His name was changed to Abednego meaning 'servant of Nato'; who is also a god. They were all given pagan names when they came into Babylonian captivity. Typically, today when they are referred to their pagan names are used. More appropriately they should be referred to as either the three Hebrew boys or by their Hebrew names. When one switches to using their pagan names, they are not identifying who they are at the core, reverencing God.

Daniel was given favor with the master of the eunuchs. He asked that they not eat the king's meat because they had purposed in their heart not to defile themselves. They were granted their request and this exception was granting them favor. They asked if they could eat the fruit of the ground. The captain thought that if they were permitted to eat what they requested their countenance would look bad. They agreed that if their appearance looked bad they would obey the original request; but their countenance looked better. Notice the Bible indicates they had to be without blemish. They had to have all knowledge and understanding. They had to be the cream of the crop (Daniel 1:4). Daniel and his three Hebrew friends, were the best of the best. Yes, we remember them going into the fiery furnace; and God showing up in the furnace. We read that Nebuchadnezzar remarked about throwing three men bound into the furnace but seeing four men and they were loosed. The appearance of the fourth man in the furnace was as the Son of God. Yes, they were thrown in, accompanied by Jesus, loosed inside the furnace and released. But the end says not only did they get out but they didn't even smell like smoke and they were promoted (Daniel 3:30). Now that's major favor.

Some of the richest men in the world history were believers including Job, Abraham, and Solomon. Solomon was so rich that even the Queen of Sheba came to see all that he had; and he showed her everything. He was entrusted by God to amass wealth.

If we have favor then we are living with the 'so much more'.

"And Jesus increased in wisdom and stature, and in favour with God and man." (Luke 2:52)

Even Jesus grew to have favor with God and man. When we seek the Lord, the preference is seen.

Jeremiah 33:3 the Bible says, **"Call unto me and I will answer thee and show thee great and mighty things which thou knowest not"**. If we ask the God of this entire universe, He is going to impart wisdom and knowledge. He answers us which amounts to favor. We are seeking and calling on Him and His reply is showing us great things and mighty things that others don't have the privilege of knowing.

"The young lions do lack, and suffer hunger: but they that seek the LORD shall not want any good thing." (Psalm 34:10)

They that seek – pursue after through worship - the Lord shall not long for any beneficial thing. That reminds us of the fact that the Lord is our shepherd and we shall not want for anything. If you want favor then you must seek Him.

"For the LORD God is a sun and shield: the LORD will give grace and glory: no good thing will he withhold from them that walk uprightly. O LORD of hosts, blessed is the man that trusteth in thee." (Psalm 84:11)

Wow! If we knew all of this was in the Bible we would walk around recognizing favor is coming! Our expectation would be high.

If we seek Him; He said He's going to give us grace and glory. His glory is His manifested presence. If God shows up in our worship the Bible says that at His right hand are pleasures ever more (Psalm 16:11). And He said no good thing is He going to withhold if we are walking according to His will. That promise encourages us to walk upright so that His unmerited favor and His presence abounds.

The giants of favor discussed were Joseph and Daniel. Joseph is exiled from the promised land. Daniel is exiled from his homeland. Both were forced from their land into another land. It doesn't matter where you are; God's favor will show up. Whether you are taken from your land or where you find yourself; God's favor will follow you. Both men walked after the Lord and both had no sense of inferiority. But of course, Jesus is our best example of one walking in favor.

Jesus is the greatest giant of favor. Looking at Luke 2:52, **"He grew in stature and had favor with both God and man".** He was faithful to the Father. He was obedient and submissive to His earthly parents as well. God blesses man through man. If we are going to get blessings and favor it is going to come through others here on earth.

> **"If any man serve me, let him follow me; and where I am, there shall also my servant be: if any man serve me, him will my Father honour."** *(John 12:26)*

Looking at this Scripture, we notice that Jesus said if any man continues to render assistance to me to fulfill my purposes, my Father is going to honor him. Now our desire is for the favor as well as the honor that Jesus will give. In the 17th chapter of John known as the high priestly prayer verse 22 records, **"And the glory which thou gavest me I have given them; that they may be one, even as we are one:"**

This shows Jesus praying to the Father on our behalf. He indicates that the glory which the Father gave Him He gave to us; this would be the honor. Jesus gave the glory, the manifested presence that was given to Him by the Father, to us. Since this is true and recorded, we need to walk in it. Maybe we just didn't read it or maybe we didn't fully comprehend it which requires us to slow down and read it again. For example, we will read *'Now unto him who is able to do exceeding abundantly above all we could hope ask or think according to the power that works within us'* too superficially. The power works in us! We don't think about the fact that it works *in us*. So, let's stop and make sure we see and comprehend; He has given us glory.

"For thou hast made him a little lower than the angels, and hast crowned him with glory and honour." (Psalm 8:5)

Jesus is distinguished by the Father as qualified for the dominion over the angels being given a position of authority; He was crowned with glory and honor. He is definitely our greatest giant of favor.

We've done the work to come out of poverty. We know what we must do to come to the level of prosperity which includes provision and then adding favor takes us over into abundance.

Onward to Abundance

"All the commandments which I command thee this day shall ye observe to do, that ye may live, and multiply, and go in and possess

the land which the LORD sware unto your fathers." (Deuteronomy 8:1)

God reminds the children of Israel of all that He has done for them. He delivered them from bondage in Egypt. He parted the Red Sea so they walked across on dry land. He drowned their enemies. He rained down manna from heaven to feed them. He brought them through the wilderness 40 years; their clothes didn't wear out or get old. Their shoes didn't wear out. So, they should have been eternally grateful. God warns them of amnesia regarding who did these things for them. He said don't say your hand did it. Don't say God wasn't the one that did it. Verse 18 records, **"The Lord is the one that gives you the power to get wealth"**. If God did not give us the mind that we have we would not have our jobs. If He did not give us the strength that we have we could not work on those jobs. So, when we recognize that God is the one that is giving us breath in our bodies, activities of our limbs, a mind that is able to process, we recognize He is the one that is giving us the power to get wealth. We don't want to forget that nor forget God.

There is a reason why He gives us the power; He wants to establish His covenant. This is done so that the world recognizes that you are His children. The world should see that there is something different between you and them. God gives you the means to hold your job. There are testimonies of receiving jobs that you didn't deserve; weren't qualified. Jobs you didn't even know existed; but somebody called you to apply and already had it set up. That's favor. That's God showing up in your life saying that He is able to supply all your needs. He gives you power. He gives you the means to get riches.

We acknowledge God as the source. If He is the source giving us the wealth, it is easier for us to release it. We put all things in proper perspective. As a steward we are just a manager; it is not ours. So, God establishes His covenant and He shows us favor therefore we need to look at the principle of contentment.

CONTENTMENT
- Being satisfied with a state (not complacency)
- Auto-sufficient, self sufficient with Christ in you

COVETOUSNESS
- The opposite of contentment
- The desire to have something for oneself that belongs to another – a craving or passionate desire
- Inordinate desire to have more

Principle of Contentment

Contentment refers to being satisfied with a state. It means to be comfortable with your current position; but not complacent. Complacency comes with the understanding of being without motivation to move. The opposite of contentment is covetousness.

> *"Let as many servants as are under the yoke count their own masters worthy of all honour, that the name of God and his doctrine be not blasphemed. And they that have believing masters, let them not despise them, because they are brethren; but rather do them service, because they are faithful and beloved, partakers of the benefit. These things teach and exhort. If any man teach otherwise, and consent not to wholesome words, even the words of our Lord Jesus Christ, and to the doctrine which is according to godliness; He is proud, knowing nothing, but doting about questions and strifes of words, whereof cometh envy, strife, railings, evil surmisings, Perverse disputings of men of corrupt minds, and destitute of the truth, supposing that gain is godliness: from such withdraw thyself. But godliness with contentment is great gain. For we brought nothing into this world, and it is certain we can carry nothing out. And having food and raiment let us be therewith content. But they that will be rich fall into temptation and a snare, and into many foolish and hurtful lusts, which drown men in destruction and perdition. For the love of money is the root of all evil: which while some coveted after, they have erred from the faith, and*

pierced themselves through with many sorrows. But thou, O man of God, flee these things; and follow after righteousness, godliness, faith, love, patience, meekness. Fight the good fight of faith, lay hold on eternal life, whereunto thou art also called, and hast professed a good profession before many witnesses. I give thee charge in the sight of God, who quickeneth all things, and before Christ Jesus, who before Pontius Pilate witnessed a good confession; That thou keep this commandment without spot, unrebukeable, until the appearing of our Lord Jesus Christ: Which in his times he shall shew, who is the blessed and only Potentate, the King of kings, and Lord of lords; Who only hath immortality, dwelling in the light which no man can approach unto; whom no man hath seen, nor can see: to whom be honour and power everlasting. Amen. Charge them that are rich in this world, that they be not highminded, nor trust in uncertain riches, but in the living God, who giveth us richly all things to enjoy;" (1 Timothy 6:1-17)

There are some that are not followers of Christ but they are adhering to Biblical principles. There are many men who do well financially. Sowing and reaping is a principal it will produce whether you believe in God or not. If you plant a seed it is going to grow. If you water it, you take care of it, and tend to it, it is going to grow. If you happen to not believe in God but you're planting a whole lot of seeds and you have a whole lot of crops that are growing, you have amassed a multitude of money and it doesn't mean you are godly. As believers we withdraw from them if they're not giving us God's word to follow for it will not be beneficial. Verse 6, **"godliness with contentment is great gain"**. Holiness with satisfaction in the state that you are in is profitable. **"For you brought nothing into this world and it is certain we can carry nothing out."** When you were born you weren't born with a purse, ladies. And you weren't born with a man bag, guys. When the doctors spanked you on the butt that was it. That's all you had. You had to get diapers from your parents and borrow a t-shirt or onesie. Upon death it is guaranteed that the deceased person is not taking anything with them. You can write them a check but they will not be able to cash it. We will have no need for money on the other side. Having food and raiment; let us therefore be pleased.

There is a difference between being content or being satisfied with what God has given and being complacent. Contentment says that where you are you know that God is aware of your conditions. You can say, "God I know you're looking out for me, you're covering me and you have me in this place for a reason so let me learn my lesson". Let's look back at Joseph's life; he's in prison. He surely didn't want to be in prison, but we don't hear of his countenance being different. We don't hear him moaning and complaining even in jail. When we learn how to be abased (having very little) and we learn how to abound (having much) and are content (satisfied); that's the state we want to attain. It is possible that over the course of our lives we will vacillate between the two states but our aim is to be satisfied on either side.

Where I am now financially is vastly different than it was when I was growing up. As children we didn't recognize the state we were in when we had soup and sandwiches for dinner. We thought it was great; we didn't realize my mother was stretching the meal. You might not have gotten all the latest toys for Christmas, and we got quite a few, but you still had food, clothes and shelter. Most of the times children like to play with the boxes anyway; they didn't have to have the toy. What is apparent is that whether or not it was the greatest steak dinner or if your meal was soup instead; that is all you know. There was food available to eat. If you're content you say, "Lord I know you see where I am and eventually it will change." The idea is to still be satisfied where you are whether you have a surplus or not.

We didn't bring anything into the world and it is certain we can carry nothing out (1 Timothy 6:7). No one has seen a hearse with a Brinks truck following behind it; life doesn't work like that. All that we amass here on earth will remain on earth in someone else's care.

There is a story of a woman whose husband asked that she bury him with a million dollars. The day came when he died. At the funeral she was found leaning over the body. Her friend asked if she really was going to put a million dollars in the coffin. She replied, "Of course, I wrote him a check."

Verse 9 indicates that they that will be rich fall into temptation. Why? because the more you have, if you're looking to money instead of to God you have then changed your affection and your loyalty and the Bible says you can't serve two masters. The temptation is to change our loyalty and forget God.

"For the love of money is the root of all evil."
(1 Timothy 6:10a)

The passage didn't say that money is evil. It said the love of money is the root of all evil. The word love here is *phileo* which is equivalent to fondness. The desire for and craving after money is what leads to evil. It could be evil intentions, actions, or thoughts all trying to acquire money. The Bible says that we can't serve two masters. Either we depend, trust and rely on money or we depend, trust and rely on God. (Matthew 6:24; Luke 16:13)

Paul is writing to Timothy and he says charge them that are rich; instruct them that have an abundance (verse 17). That means some in the church are going to be rich; they will have a surplus. Though you may have it today, you can't count on uncertain riches. If you play the lottery, if you put money in the stock market; it's not guaranteed. You may have done well this year but there is no guarantee that you will in the future. You can't be assured you are going to be here tomorrow. What you put in your investments you can't know with confidence that it will increase or remain the same. That's why we should not trust in these uncertain riches but in the Living God. Our money says 'In God We Trust'. We trust in the living God which gives us all things to enjoy. Paul tells us also that they (the rich) do good and they invest in good works. They are ready to distribute, to assist others. They are willing to as the Bible says communicate. The word communicate is not referring to talk but it is the word *koinonia* which is fellowship. In other words, they must share with others. Looking at this passage we have to conclude that everybody is not going to be a millionaire only those favored by God. Consider the rich young ruler, Jesus said it is easier for the camel to go thru the eye of a needle than for a rich man to get into heaven. If there is a choice of being rich or going to heaven, which would you choose? Let's look closely at Mark 10:17-31

"And when he was gone forth into the way, there came one running, and kneeled to him, and asked him, Good Master, what shall I do that I may inherit eternal life? And Jesus said unto him, Why callest thou me good? there is none good but one, that is, God. Thou knowest the commandments, Do not commit adultery, Do not kill, Do not steal, Do not bear false witness, Defraud not, Honour thy father and mother. And he answered and said unto him, Master, all these have I observed from my youth. Then Jesus beholding him loved him, and said unto him, One thing thou lackest: go thy way, sell whatsoever thou

hast, and give to the poor, and thou shalt have treasure in heaven: and come, take up the cross, and follow me. And he was sad at that saying, and went away grieved: for he had great possessions. And Jesus looked round about, and saith unto his disciples, How hardly shall they that have riches enter into the kingdom of God! And the disciples were astonished at his words. But Jesus answereth again, and saith unto them, Children, how hard is it for them that trust in riches to enter into the kingdom of God! It is easier for a camel to go through the eye of a needle, than for a rich man to enter into the kingdom of God. And they were astonished out of measure, saying among themselves, Who then can be saved? And Jesus looking upon them saith, With men it is impossible, but not with God: for with God all things are possible. Then Peter began to say unto him, Lo, we have left all, and have followed thee. And Jesus answered and said, Verily I say unto you, There is no man that hath left house, or brethren, or sisters, or father, or mother, or wife, or children, or lands, for my sake, and the gospel's, But he shall receive an hundredfold now in this time, houses, and brethren, and sisters, and mothers, and children, and lands, with persecutions; and in the world to come eternal life. But many that are first shall be last; and the last first.

Now this passage doesn't say that we need to take a vow of poverty. The Bible says it is hard for one that trusts in riches to enter the kingdom of heaven. The difference is that they are putting the expectation in and relying on the riches. The one who places their faith in the money will not enter the kingdom of heaven. They play the lottery thinking they are going to get rich quick. They devise schemes and possibly end up doing something illegal. Giving to the church with funds obtained illegally does not absolve one from the act and is inappropriate. Difficult circumstances should not lead to illegal actions but requires that we learn contentment. Covetousness is an issue if you have an affection or insatiable desire for more money since it is the root of all evil. Why? because the more you get, you start forgetting God. It can be seen today in not waiting to get the house and the car but wanting it all at the wedding. It's a give it to me right now attitude. It can be seen in the Robin Hood idea of taking from the rich and giving to the poor (for covetous reasons only); the rich should pay more in taxes and give to meet my lack. If you don't have enough it may be a budget issue. If you spend more than you earn it very likely is an issue of not being able to handle what you have. It also may indicate you are not prepared for the future. You may squander what income you do have. Most of the lottery winners have ended up broke busted and disgusted because they didn't know how to handle the influx of money. They ended up with nothing. The principles are very important; don't be covetous. More money thrown at a situation usually does not solve the problem.

If one trusts in riches he is not then depending on God. So, the trust is misplaced; and that's why they would not get into heaven. If the trust or hope is in the money then one is trying to make it for himself. You're trying hard with a plan A and plan B and you create what you think is a safety net. Instead of considering the Lord as your shepherd so you shall not want and rehearsing that you've never seen the righteous forsaken nor his seed begging bread; you rely on your own works and effort.

You can be content and still desire to have more; but you want that more as you seek the Lord. You want what God wants you to have; because if He has a work for you to do then He is going to supply what you need. He doesn't give a vision without the provision.

We like to quote Hebrews 13:5 where God said He will never leave us nor forsake us but we forget the first part. God says**, "Let your conversation (your behavior) be without covetous (desiring of what somebody else has) but be content with such as you have (Hebrews 13:5a, clarifications mine)."** Your behavior is your lifestyle. It is how you walk and carry yourself. We are admonished to be content and not covet. Covetousness was the problem that Satan had from the beginning.

> *"The word of the LORD came again unto me, saying, Son of man, say unto the prince of Tyrus, Thus saith the Lord GOD; Because thine heart is lifted up, and thou hast said, I*

am a God, I sit in the seat of God, in the midst of the seas; yet thou art a man, and not God, though thou set thine heart as the heart of God: Behold, thou art wiser than Daniel; there is no secret that they can hide from thee: With thy wisdom and with thine understanding thou hast gotten thee riches, and hast gotten gold and silver into thy treasures: By thy great wisdom and by thy traffick hast thou increased thy riches, and thine heart is lifted up because of thy riches: Therefore thus saith the Lord GOD; Because thou hast set thine heart as the heart of God; Behold, therefore I will bring strangers upon thee, the terrible of the nations: and they shall draw their swords against the beauty of thy wisdom, and they shall defile thy brightness. They shall bring thee down to the pit, and thou shalt die the deaths of them that are slain in the midst of the seas. Wilt thou yet say before him that slayeth thee, I am God? but thou shalt be a man, and no God, in the hand of him that slayeth thee. Thou shalt die the deaths of the uncircumcised by the hand of strangers: for I have spoken it, saith the Lord GOD. Moreover the word of the LORD came unto me, saying, Son of man, take up a lamentation upon the king of Tyrus, and say unto him, Thus saith the Lord GOD; Thou sealest up the sum, full of wisdom, and perfect in beauty. Thou hast been in Eden the garden of God; every precious stone was thy

covering, the sardius, topaz, and the diamond, the beryl, the onyx, and the jasper, the sapphire, the emerald, and the carbuncle, and gold: the workmanship of thy tabrets and of thy pipes was prepared in thee in the day that thou wast created. Thou art the anointed cherub that covereth; and I have set thee so: thou wast upon the holy mountain of God; thou hast walked up and down in the midst of the stones of fire. Thou wast perfect in thy ways from the day that thou wast created, till iniquity was found in thee. By the multitude of thy merchandise they have filled the midst of thee with violence, and thou hast sinned: therefore I will cast thee as profane out of the mountain of God: and I will destroy thee, O covering cherub, from the midst of the stones of fire. Thine heart was lifted up because of thy beauty, thou hast corrupted thy wisdom by reason of thy brightness: I will cast thee to the ground, I will lay thee before kings, that they may behold thee. Thou hast defiled thy sanctuaries by the multitude of thine iniquities, by the iniquity of thy traffick; therefore will I bring forth a fire from the midst of thee, it shall devour thee, and I will bring thee to ashes upon the earth in the sight of all them that behold thee. All they that know thee among the people shall be astonished at thee: thou shalt be a terror, and never shalt thou be any more."
(Ezekiel 28:1-19)

In this passage we identify both Tyrus, an earthly king, and Satan. As we look at Tyrus and the switch to Satan we recognize both were not satisfied with what they had but they wanted more. It is the same spirit. God indicates that Satan's heart was lifted up because of the riches. The Bible records that it was because of his trafficking and his merchandising (his buying and selling) that he was cast down. Satan was desiring to have more; more of the authority, more power, more honor, and that equates to covetousness. He wanted the glory and honor only reserved for God. Covetousness indicates a desire to have what somebody else has and that was the original problem. His desire was to get more than he had though he had everything; he wasn't content. He thought more highly of himself than he ought to think and wanted to position himself in the place of God.

Every precious stone was his covering and the authority he had was represented by the term 'the cherub that covers'. Cherubs were not cute little babies as displayed today. For a clearer picture see the description in Genesis 3:24. Covering indicates that he had a position of authority. Every precious stone, all the gems, were in him. He was the anointed and given a position of honor and power. Satan's first sin was this covetousness; he was adorned with authority but his desire was for more. Why he would desire more is almost incomprehensible. God had given him authority and brilliant stones yet he wanted more. Covetousness wants what others have.

"Let your character or moral disposition be free from love of money [including greed, avarice, lust, and craving for earthly possessions] and be satisfied with your present [circumstances and with what you have]; for He [God] Himself has said, I will not in any way fail you nor give you up nor leave you without support. [I will} not, [I will] not, [I will] not in any degree leave you helpless nor forsake nor let [you] down (relax My hold on you)! [Assuredly not!]" (Hebrews 13:5, AMP)

God says He's not going to leave you without support, forsake you, not allow you to be helpless and not give up on you however, it requires that you are content (satisfied that God is able and trustworthy). If He promises, you know when you call upon Him (Jeremiah 33:3), He's going to answer you; He's not going to withhold any good thing from you. If He's not going to leave you on your own then if you lost your job; He can open doors that no man can shut and shut doors that no man can open. If you recognize that your trust is in Him and He's not going to fail you; you rest in that confidence. If He's not going to leave you, He's not going to relax His hold on you; you rest in His trust. If He always has you in the palm of His hand then you remain content where you are. **"Godliness with contentment is great gain (1 Timothy 6:6)."** God sees your heart. He will bless you!

In the book of Exodus, one of the commandments given to us was to not covet (Exodus 20:17). If your heart is content with such that you have and you don't desire or lust after what belongs to someone else then covetousness is not your issue and you can move onward to abundance.

Abundance is prosperity and wealth, not just provision. Deuteronomy 8:18, *"But thou shalt remember the LORD thy God: for it is he that giveth thee power to get wealth, that he may establish his covenant which he sware unto thy fathers, as it is this day."* God gives us the ability to achieve riches. We should always remember that when we go to our jobs and we have funds that come in from those jobs, it is God that gives us the breath to breathe as well as the strength and the mind to do the job. He gives us the means to procure wealth and then He confirms His Covenant with us. Look back at the first verse of Deuteronomy chapter 8, *"When you observe to do that you may live and multiply and go in and possess the land which the Lord swear to your father."* Notice we have to keep all of the listed commands. We take note with the intent to follow.

"Those things, which ye have both learned, and received, and heard, and seen in me, do: and the God of peace shall be with you. But I rejoiced in the Lord greatly, that now at the last your care of me hath flourished again; wherein ye were also careful, but ye lacked opportunity. Not that I speak in respect of want: for I have learned, in whatsoever state I am, therewith to be content. I know both how

to be abased, and I know how to abound: every where and in all things I am instructed both to be full and to be hungry, both to abound and to suffer need. I can do all things through Christ which strengtheneth me." (Philippians 4:9-13)

Paul said I know how to be abased and how to abound; content in whatever state that I am in. We like to quote verse 13 but look at where it occurs; within context it is after the abasement and the abounding. After both extremes then Paul notes he and we by extension can do all things through Christ. We can eat the soup and sandwiches that we can afford while we desire to give our children more. It is only for a moment that we need to sacrifice until such time as God blesses us to get out of that situation. The definition of contentment is auto-sufficient, sufficient in Christ in you. Paul says of the Philippians, because you gave me once before or because you just lacked opportunity I learned to be satisfied. In the 11th verse Paul was not in need but he identifies that regardless of his situation or circumstance he learned contentment. Learn in the Greek language is either *nosko* meaning knowing or *epigonosko* meaning understanding and learning based on experience. There is satisfaction regardless of Paul's position or what he has coming in and going out; He has learned this mystery by initiation. If he had never been abased he would not know how to be content in that position. If he never had abundance without allowing those riches to reshape his thinking he would not have learned the lesson fully. If the thinking had changed based on riches, thinking more highly of himself than he ought, a fall could have been imminent (vs. 13). Remember Hebrews 13:5, God's not going to fail you, He's not going to relax his hold on you or let you go no matter what you're dealing with; He's got you and He covers you. If He has to, He will slap those trying to mess with you and all you have to do is duck. The Wuest translation of Philippians 4:13 says, *"I am strong for all things through the one who constantly infuses His strength into me."* Like a light bulb, when you turn it on it will light as long as there is power. That power for us as believers is Christ. IT is a continual supply that pours strength into us. Philippians 4:13 in the amplified records, *"I have strength for all things in Christ Who empowers me [I am ready for anything and equal to anything through Him Who infuses inner strength into me; I am self-sufficient in Christ's sufficiency]."*

In Corinthians Paul records, *"My grace is sufficient for you for my strength is made perfect in your weakness." (2 Corinthians 12:9)* How to be content can be as easy as recognizing God has no limitations. His strength is all that we need for any situation.

Limitations

We have no limitations except for ignorance, unbelief and flesh. Ignorance can be as simple as not knowing or reference the fact that people are destroyed for a lack of knowledge. Unbelief, not being fully persuaded that God's word is true. The flesh – what you want, think or feel- limits you in action by your motivation. We in our flesh set up boundaries that don't allow us to fully achieve everything God has for us. However, regardless of our inability to attain, God has no restrictions on His ability. How do you know that God has no limitations? Luke 1:37 *"For with God nothing shall be impossible."*

There is absolutely nothing that God can't do except fail and lie. He can make a way out of no way. He'll create whatever is necessary. If He can speak 'let there be light' separating light from the darkness and then gather up the water so that they made the dry land; He can do anything. If He parted the Red Sea, He can part your wallet too. If He worked miracles in the past; the future miracles are just a prayer away. If He caused walls to fall; He can break down any barrier. Nothing is impossible for the Almighty God.

We as individuals are a different story. One of the reasons we are limited unfortunately is ignorance. We don't know what the Word promises and we don't take the time to glean the Scriptures to find out. The Bible records that people are destroyed (come to ruin) for a lack of knowledge (Hosea 4:6). If there was stored a vault that had your name attached to it and the vault was filled to capacity with money. If you didn't know it existed you would never utilize the funds. Ignorance equates to ignoring all the benefits God has identified by burying your head in the sand. Hosea 4:6 goes on to say that the people rejected the knowledge they did have. They came to ruin because they didn't fully comprehend and accept what was available.

"And Jesus said unto them, Because of your unbelief: for verily I say unto you, If ye have faith as a grain of mustard seed, ye shall say unto this mountain, Remove hence to yonder place; and it shall remove; and nothing shall be impossible unto you." (Matthew 17:20)

A father brought his son with epilepsy to the disciples and the disciples were trying to heal him and it didn't happen. Jesus shows up and the father says to Jesus desperately, *"If you can do anything please help." (Mark 9:14-29)* Jesus replies that all things are possible to those that believe. The father admits he believes but need help with his unbelief; somewhere I'm missing it, I'm not getting it 100%. At least he realized his lack. The expectation wasn't the 'without a doubt belief' so it was unbelief. Capernaum was Jesus' headquarters and He said that he could not do many miracles there because of their unbelief (Matthew 13:58). Can you imagine the son of God being in your city and the people in the city doubting His ability and His willingness resulting in Him only healing a few sick? That's why He had a 'Woe' to them too as recorded in Matthew 25. All they needed was faith the size of a grain of a mustard seed. The mustard seed is the tiniest seed; however, it grows into a giant tree. He's giving the example that just a little bit of faith can move mountains.

Your limitations are the only thing holding you back from all God has for you. These come in the form of what you don't know, what you do not remember or what you don't believe. The promises God gives are there so that our faith can be built by meditating on the Word. We want to make sure we walk in favor. Favor is received from God through fellowship and renewing our mind. It is also received from others by faith and sowing. We must confess favor with God and man and not accept the past as a rule for the future. God promises us favor so let's stand on the promises!

> **Scriptural Ways to Achieve Abundance Bible Study Page 225**

Chapter 7: Covenant

Welcome to the throne room of God. It's the place He invites us to come worship. He makes promises, encompasses us with His love and tells us we are His. The whole world is in His hands and His protection and provision are laid in front of our lives. He breaks bread with us and makes covenant with us.

A covenant is a formal alliance or agreement made by God with a religious community or with humanity in general. It can further be defined as a binding or establishing of a relationship between two parties. This agreement God makes includes great promises with requirements. Because God is able to do anything, whatever promises He makes, He can back. The stronger party, God, makes the rules of the covenant.

The beauty is that we serve a God who has our best interest at heart, after all He gave His only Son to redeem us. Relationship with the designer of this entire universe is the best connection we could ever have. Who wouldn't want to keep an agreement that is so one sided in our favor? Meeting the requirements of this covenant ensures that the promises are not only

> **COVENANT**
> — an agreement between two people or two groups that involves promises on the part of each to the other. The Hebrew word for "covenant" probably means "betweenness," emphasizing the relational element that lies at the basis of all covenants. Human covenants or treaties were either between equals or between a superior and an inferior. Divine covenants, however, are always of the latter type, and the concept of covenant between God and His people is one of the most important theological truths of the Bible. Indeed, the word itself has come to denote the two main divisions of Christian Scripture: Old Covenant and New Covenant (traditionally, Old Testament and New Testament). Youngblood, R. F., Bruce, F. F., & Harrison, R. K., Thomas Nelson Publishers (Eds.). (1995). In <u>Nelson's new illustrated Bible dictionary</u>. <u>Nashville, TN: Thomas Nelson, Inc.</u>
>
> - the instrument constituting the rule (or kingdom) of God, and therefore it is a valuable lens through which one can recognize and appreciate the biblical ideal of religious community. Mendenhall, G. E., & Herion, G. A. (1992). <u>Covenant. In D. N. Freedman (Ed.)</u>, <u>The Anchor Yale Bible Dictionary (Vol. 1, p. 1179). New York: Doubleday.</u>

available but guaranteed. What is the covenant requirement as it relates to finances?

Tithing

> **TITHE**
> Tenth part of ones increase contributed voluntarily in support of the church and its God appointed leaders.

Tithe is defined as a tenth part of ones increase contributed voluntarily in support of the church and its God appointed leaders. Notice in the definition it highlights the heart behind it and the reason it is given. The heart motive is one that is based on love and not compulsion. God doesn't hold a gun to our heads forcing us to return the tithe. The love relationship of our covenant should draw us to desire the secret place of safety and protection of all that He gives us. The benefactors of the tithe include the leaders serving and those that the church assists. Support of the church and its leaders is also called storehouse tithing by some and require that it be given to the local church. In Malachi 3:10 the Bible says, *"bring all the tithes into the storehouse so that there might be meat in my house and prove me now."* There is a difference between a tithe and a present that is offered up. A present or tribute is synonymous with the words gift, sacrificial gift, heave offering or oblation. The distinction between supporting the local assembly and its leaders with a specific amount and a gift offered without stipulation are usually identified on our giving envelopes. There is a distinction also between tithe and offering. Our participation in each says a lot about our love walk. If we love God like we say we do, Is our checkbook or bank account deductions reflective of our heart?

As we look at the tithe, there are key dispensation times in history that we will investigate. The principle of the tithe which occurs under Abraham; the law of the tithe directed through Moses; and then there is the grace of the tithe which is under Jesus Christ.

The Principle of the Tithe

"Now the LORD had said unto Abram, Get thee out of thy country, and from thy kindred, and from thy father's house, unto a land that I will shew thee: And I will make of thee a great nation, and I will bless thee, and make thy name great; and thou shalt be a blessing: And I will bless them that bless thee, and curse him that curseth thee: and in thee shall all families of the earth be blessed." (Genesis 12:1-3)

This covenant stated between God and Abram sets the stage for all the promises and blessings for all generations. There is the protection of ensuring that whatever comes God will meet head on, on behalf of Abram. God said he was going to make Abram a great nation. God blessed him to be a blessing and anybody that blesses Abram, God will bless and anyone who curses Abram, God will curse.

The blessing by definition is speaking well of someone. It carries with it the understanding that good spoken over an individual will be performed by the blesser. Since God spoke and the world was formed, when He speaks the winds and the waves obey. What God speaks over our lives shall come to pass by His power. God speaks the covenant and keeps the covenant with Abram making his descendants as the sands on the sea shore, and the stars in the sky. Innumerable in quantity and impactful in quality are the sons and daughters of Abraham. Blessings flow from those aligned as family members to generations waiting to be engrafted into the family. This covenant continues today with God blessing us and doing so that we bless others.

> *"For all the land which thou seest, to thee will I give it, and to thy seed for ever. And I will make thy seed as the dust of the earth: so that if a man can number the dust of the earth, then shall thy seed also be numbered." (Genesis 13:15,16)*

With the awesome commitment of the covenant Abram sojourns winning battles by the power of God. He has the protection and the victory of the God of the universe wherever he goes. In Genesis 14:17-20, we encounter an exchange between Abram and God's representative.

"And the king of Sodom went out to meet him after his return from the slaughter of Chedorlaomer, and of the kings that were with him, at the valley of Shaveh, which is the king's dale. And Melchizedek king of Salem brought forth bread and wine: and he was the priest of the most high God. And he blessed him, and said, Blessed be Abram of the most high God, possessor of heaven and earth: And blessed be the most high God, which hath delivered thine enemies into thy hand. And he gave him tithes of all." (Genesis 14:17-20)

Abram gave a tithe to Melchizedek who is the priest of the most high God. A priest stands before the people as a representative for God. This is giving of a tithe is significant as the first time this is established; it shows the original intent. Melchizedek stands before Abram at the conclusion of his battle. When one goes to war the prevailing party gets to take the spoils of war. The gold, the silver, whatever spoils are captured the victor takes them as their possession. Abram confiscates all but instead he takes a tenth of all of what he gained and he gives it to Melchizedek. At this point his offering is offered in the spirit of giving because there is no law yet. It was a sacrificial heart acknowledgement of the covenant and God fulfilling His promise. God hasn't established the law of the tithe which is given in a later dispensation. This tithe (a tenth part) is given because Abram recognized that God had him prevail and be victorious in the battle.

Hebrews 7:4-10 is going to parallel this account because the writer of Hebrews is an unknown second-generation believer. These believers are going to know the Old Testament so it is referenced in order that they can follow the progression from the Old Testament to the New Testament.

> *"Now consider how great this man was, unto whom even the patriarch Abraham gave the tenth of the spoils. And verily they that are of the sons of Levi, who receive the office of the priesthood, have a commandment to take tithes of the people according to the law, that is, of their brethren, though they come out of the loins of Abraham: But he whose descent is not counted from them received tithes of Abraham, and blessed him that had the promises. And without all contradiction the less is blessed of the better. And here men that die receive tithes; but there he receiveth them, of whom it is witnessed that he liveth. And as I may so say, Levi also, who receiveth tithes, payed tithes in Abraham. For he was yet in the loins of his father, when Melchisedec met him." (Hebrews 7:4-10)*

He's referring to the fact that Abraham (Abram in Genesis because God had not changed his name yet) had descendants that were giving because of his gift. Abraham was passing on the principle to his family. Melchisedec (Melchizedek in Hebrew spelling) being the king of Salem; Salem with the Hebrew root word being *shalom*. *Shalom* meaning perfect and whole peace. He is the king of the city of peace. This word is used also in Psalm 76:2 and has been interpreted to be a reference to Jerusalem (Yaruwshalayim- Hebrew Strong's #3389- founded in peace). In Hebrews 7:1-3 we get more information on Melchisedec:

> *"For this Melchisedec, king of Salem, priest of the most high God, who met Abraham returning from the slaughter of the kings, and blessed him; To whom also Abraham gave a tenth part of all; first being by interpretation King of righteousness, and after that also King of Salem, which is, King of peace; Without father, without mother, without descent, having neither beginning of days, nor end of life; but made like unto the Son of God; abideth a priest continually."*

Melchisedec is identified as the King of Righteousness, the King of Salem. He is made a priest continually; without cessation. As priest he stands in the gap between God and the people. Melchisedec received the tithe from Abraham as well as from his seed (descendants) yet to come. The principal was set. He acknowledges God as a covenant keeper and out of that relationship he brought a tithe to honor Him.

"After these things the word of the LORD came unto Abram in a vision, saying, Fear not, Abram: I am thy shield, and thy exceeding great reward." (Genesis 15:1)

God continued expounding on His covenant with Abram by promising to be his protection and his reward. Not just any reward does he promise but his exceeding great reward. Looking up exceeding, we find that it means fast and rapid. Great says that the reward is ever-increasing. And the word reward refers to salary, wages and money supply. As God makes the covenant with Abraham He declares that He will speak well of him and his descendants making him a great nation. God continues by stating He will be Abraham's fast ever increase in salary; his rapid ever-increasing money supply. When Abraham then meets up with Melchisedec it is easy for him to give a tenth because God in covenant will supply. You are my wages, you are my salary, you are all that I need; these are the sentiments of Abraham based on God's declaration.

"For I know him, that he will command his children and his household after him, and they shall keep the way of the LORD, to do justice and judgment; that the LORD may bring upon Abraham that which he hath spoken of him." (Genesis 18:19)

God's covenant with Abraham declares that he (Abraham) will keep the commandments of God and he will tell his children. The principal that Abraham walks in and establishes, he then will teach it to his descendants and God knows this in advance. As we looked at Hebrews 7 we saw that Levi payed tithes in Abraham as he was in his father's loins. Continuing through the Scriptures we find this principle manifesting in the lives of Abraham's descendants including Isaac, Jacob, David and Solomon.

"And there was a famine in the land, beside the first famine that was in the days of Abraham. And Isaac went unto Abimelech king of the Philistines unto Gerar." (Genesis 26:1)

"Then Isaac sowed in that land, and received in the same year an hundredfold: and the LORD blessed him." (Genesis 26:12)

The conditions of his situation, whether famine or prosperity, did not change his commitment to return the tithe under the principle established by Abraham. Isaac's resolve like his father Abraham was to acknowledge God by returning a tenth portion of all his increase to God regardless of famine or dirth or drought.

"And Jacob went out from Beersheba, and went toward Haran. And he lighted upon a certain place, and tarried there all night,

because the sun was set; and he took of the stones of that place, and put them for his pillows, and lay down in that place to sleep. And he dreamed, and behold a ladder set up on the earth, and the top of it reached to heaven: and behold the angels of God ascending and descending on it. And, behold, the LORD stood above it, and said, I am the LORD God of Abraham thy father, and the God of Isaac: the land whereon thou liest, to thee will I give it, and to thy seed; And thy seed shall be as the dust of the earth, and thou shalt spread abroad to the west, and to the east, and to the north, and to the south: and in thee and in thy seed shall all the families of the earth be blessed. And, behold, I am with thee, and will keep thee in all places whither thou goest, and will bring thee again into this land; for I will not leave thee, until I have done that which I have spoken to thee of. And Jacob awaked out of his sleep, and he said, Surely the LORD is in this place; and I knew it not. And he was afraid, and said, How dreadful is this place! this is none other but the house of God, and this is the gate of heaven. And Jacob rose up early in the morning, and took the stone that he had put for his pillows, and set it up for a pillar, and poured oil upon the top of it. And he called the name of that place Bethel: but the name of that city was called Luz at the first." (Genesis 28:10-19)

Jacob gave an oil offering as he poured it on top of the altar he built to acknowledge God.

"My son, forget not my law; but let thine heart keep my commandments: For length of days, and long life, and peace, shall they add to thee. Let not mercy and truth forsake thee: bind them about thy neck; write them upon the table of thine heart: So shalt thou find favour and good understanding in the sight of God and man. Trust in the LORD with all thine heart; and lean not unto thine own understanding. In all thy ways acknowledge him, and he shall direct thy paths. Be not wise in thine own eyes: fear the LORD, and depart from evil. It shall be health to thy navel, and marrow to thy bones. Honour the LORD with thy substance, and with the firstfruits of all thine increase: So shall thy barns be filled with plenty, and thy presses shall burst out with new wine." (Proverbs 3:1-10)

As David followed after the God of Abraham, Isaac and Jacob, he continued the principle that we see acknowledged by his son Solomon in Proverbs. The admonition is to honor the Lord with your substance.

"In Gibeon the LORD appeared to Solomon in a dream by night: and God said, Ask what I shall give thee. And Solomon said, Thou hast shewed unto thy servant David my father

great mercy, according as he walked before thee in truth, and in righteousness, and in uprightness of heart with thee; and thou hast kept for him this great kindness, that thou hast given him a son to sit on his throne, as it is this day. And now, O LORD my God, thou hast made thy servant king instead of David my father: and I am but a little child: I know not how to go out or come in. And thy servant is in the midst of thy people which thou hast chosen, a great people, that cannot be numbered nor counted for multitude. Give therefore thy servant an understanding heart to judge thy people, that I may discern between good and bad: for who is able to judge this thy so great a people?" (1 Kings 3:5-9)

"And Solomon awoke; and, behold, it was a dream. And he came to Jerusalem, and stood before the ark of the covenant of the LORD, and offered up burnt offerings, and offered peace offerings, and made a feast to all his servants." (1 Kings 3:15)

Solomon continues the giving acknowledging that his father David had also taught him the covenant. Solomon offers burnt offerings, peace offerings and a feast. The giving of the descendants of Abraham continues.

"Now Jericho was straitly shut up because of the children of Israel: none went out, and none came in. And the LORD said unto Joshua, See, I have given into thine hand Jericho, and the king thereof, and the mighty men of valour. And ye shall compass the city, all ye men of war, and go round about the city once. Thus shalt thou do six days. And seven priests shall bear before the ark seven trumpets of rams' horns: and the seventh day ye shall compass the city seven times, and the priests shall blow with the trumpets. And it shall come to pass, that when they make a long blast with the ram's horn, and when ye hear the sound of the trumpet, all the people shall shout with a great shout; and the wall of the city shall fall down flat, and the people shall ascend up every man straight before him. And Joshua the son of Nun called the priests, and said unto them, Take up the ark of the covenant, and let seven priests bear seven trumpets of rams' horns before the ark of the LORD. And he said unto the people, Pass on, and compass the city, and let him that is armed pass on before the ark of the LORD. And it came to pass, when Joshua had spoken unto the people, that the seven priests bearing the seven trumpets of rams' horns passed on before the LORD, and blew with the trumpets: and the ark of the covenant of the LORD followed them. And the armed men went before the priests that blew with the trumpets, and the rereward came after the ark, the priests going on, and blowing with the trumpets. And Joshua had commanded the people, saying, Ye shall not shout, nor make any noise with your voice, neither shall any word proceed out of your mouth, until the day I bid you shout; then shall ye shout. So the ark of the LORD compassed the city, going about it once: and they came into the camp, and lodged in the camp. And Joshua rose early in the morning, and the priests took up the ark of the LORD. And seven priests bearing seven trumpets of rams' horns before the ark of the LORD went on continually, and blew with the trumpets: and the armed men went before them; but the rereward came after the ark of the LORD, the priests going on, and blowing with the trumpets. And the second day they compassed the city once, and returned into the camp: so they did six days. And it came to pass on the seventh day, that they rose early about the dawning of the day, and compassed the city after the same manner seven times: only on that day they compassed the city seven times. And it came to pass at the seventh time, when the priests blew with the trumpets, Joshua said unto the people, Shout; for the LORD hath given you the city. And the city shall be accursed, even it, and all that are therein, to the LORD: only Rahab the harlot shall live, she and all that are with her *in the house, because she hid the messengers that we sent. And ye, in any wise keep yourselves from the accursed thing, lest ye make yourselves accursed, when ye take of the accursed thing, and make the camp of Israel a curse, and trouble it. But all the silver, and gold, and vessels of brass and iron, are consecrated unto the LORD: they shall come into the treasury of the LORD. So the people shouted when the priests blew with the trumpets: and it came to pass, when the people heard the sound of the trumpet, and the people shouted with a great shout, that the wall fell down flat, so that the people went up into the city, every man straight before him, and they took the city. And they utterly destroyed all that was in the city, both man and woman, young and old, and ox, and sheep, and ass, with the edge of the sword. But Joshua had said unto the two men that had spied out the country, Go into the harlot's house, and bring out thence the woman, and all that she hath, as ye sware unto her. And the young men that were spies went in, and brought out Rahab, and her father, and her mother, and her brethren, and all that she had; and they brought out all her kindred, and left them without the camp of Israel. And they burnt the city with fire, and all that was therein: only the silver, and the gold, and the vessels of brass and of iron, they put into the treasury of the house of the LORD. And*

Joshua saved Rahab the harlot alive, and her father's household, and all that she had; and she dwelleth in Israel even unto this day; because she hid the messengers, which Joshua sent to spy out Jericho. And Joshua adjured them at that time, saying, Cursed be the man before the LORD, that riseth up and buildeth this city Jericho: he shall lay the foundation thereof in his firstborn, and in his youngest son shall he set up the gates of it. So the LORD was with Joshua; and his fame was noised throughout all the country."
(Joshua 6:1-27)

Joshua hearing from the Lord and reminded of the covenant God made, went to battle and won. The passage identifies that the Lord was with Joshua. From the spoils, ten percent (10%) of that first portion received is given to the Lord because of appreciation for God and His blessings not because of a law. Originally the tithe was an appreciative gift given to God's representative.

As a note, Melchisedec is a type of Christ as the Bible does identify him as a high priest forever after the order of Melchizedek. Type represents a pre-incarnate appearance. Jesus is also referred to as the Prince of Peace (Isaiah 9:6) as well as a King (Matthew 2:2; 27:37; Mark 15:2,38: Luke 23:2,38: John 1:49; 18:37; 1 Timothy 1:17, Revelation 19:16) and Priest (Hebrews 3:1; 4:14,15; 7:3,15; 8:1; 9:11). A character study on Melchisedec would show many similarities and add a wealth of understanding to the priesthood and kingship of Christ.

Note the spelling differences of Melchisedec's (Melchizedek's) name relate to whether it is Hebrew or Greek. If you look it up in the Strong's Concordance you will see it references the same person.

> *"In keeping with [the oath's greater strength and force], Jesus has become the Guarantee of a better (stronger) agreement [a more excellent and more advantageous covenant]. [Again, the former successive line of priests] was made up of many, because they were each prevented by death from continuing [perpetually in office]; But He holds His priesthood unchangeably, because He lives on forever. Therefore He is able to save to the uttermost; (completely, perfectly, finally, and for all time and eternity) those who come to God through Him, since He is always living to make petition to God and intercede with Him and intervene for them. [Here is] the High Priest [perfectly adapted] to our needs, as was fitting holy, blameless, unstained by sin, separated from sinners, and exalted higher than the heavens. He has no day by day necessity, as [do each of these other] high priests, to offer sacrifice first of all for his own [personal] sins and then for those of the people, because He [met all the requirements] once for all when He brought Himself [as a*

sacrifice] which He offered up." (Hebrews 7:22-27, AMP)

"For unto us a child is born, unto us a son is given: and the government shall be upon his shoulder: and his name shall be called Wonderful, Counsellor, The mighty God, The everlasting Father, The Prince of Peace." (Isaiah 9:6)

"For in Him the whole fullness of Deity (the Godhead) continues to dwell in bodily form [giving complete expression of the divine nature]. And you are in Him, made full and having come to fullness of life [in Christ you too are filled with the Godhead – Father, Son and Holy Spirit- and reach full spiritual stature]. And He is the Head of all rule and authority [of every angelic principality and power}." (Colossians 2:9-10, AMP)

The Law of the Tithe

The book of Deuteronomy is the second law for the new generation. Moses broke the original tablets God made which detailed the commandments when he found that the people had already broken them. In Deuteronomy the 5th chapter through the 26th chapter it records the covenant between God and the children of Israel. This second iteration gives more details than the 10 commandments in Exodus and actually documents 613 commandments. The 28th chapter gives us the blessing of the covenant.

"And it shall come to pass, if thou shalt hearken diligently unto the voice of the LORD thy God, to observe and to do all his commandments which I command thee this day, that the LORD thy God will set thee on high above all nations of the earth: 2 And all these blessings shall come on thee, and overtake thee, if thou shalt hearken unto the voice of the LORD thy God. Blessed shalt thou be in the city, and blessed shalt thou be in the field. Blessed shall be the fruit of thy body, and the fruit of thy ground, and the fruit of thy cattle, the increase of thy kine, and the flocks of thy sheep. Blessed shall be thy basket and thy store. Blessed shalt thou be when thou comest in, and blessed shalt thou be when thou goest out. The LORD shall cause thine enemies that rise up against thee to be smitten before thy face: they shall come out against thee one way, and flee before thee seven ways. The LORD shall command the blessing upon thee in thy storehouses, and in all that thou settest thine hand unto; and he shall bless thee in the land which the LORD thy God giveth thee. The LORD shall establish thee an holy people unto himself, as he hath sworn unto thee, if thou shalt keep the commandments of the LORD thy God, and walk in his ways. And all people of the

earth shall see that thou art called by the name of the LORD; and they shall be afraid of thee. And the LORD shall make thee plenteous in goods, in the fruit of thy body, and in the fruit of thy cattle, and in the fruit of thy ground, in the land which the LORD sware unto thy fathers to give thee. The LORD shall open unto thee his good treasure, the heaven to give the rain unto thy land in his season, and to bless all the work of thine hand: and thou shalt lend unto many nations, and thou shalt not borrow. And the LORD shall make thee the head, and not the tail; and thou shalt be above only, and thou shalt not be beneath; if that thou hearken unto the commandments of the LORD thy God, which I command thee this day, to observe and to do them: And thou shalt not go aside from any of the words which I command thee this day, to the right hand, or to the left, to go after other gods to serve them.

15 But it shall come to pass, if thou wilt not hearken unto the voice of the LORD thy God, to observe to do all his commandments and his statutes which I command thee this day; that all these curses shall come upon thee, and overtake thee: Cursed shalt thou be in the city, and cursed shalt thou be in the field. Cursed shall be thy basket and thy store. Cursed shall be the fruit of thy body, and the fruit of thy land, the increase of thy kine, and the flocks of thy sheep. Cursed shalt thou be

when thou comest in, and cursed shalt thou be when thou goest out. The LORD shall send upon thee cursing, vexation, and rebuke, in all that thou settest thine hand unto for to do, until thou be destroyed, and until thou perish quickly; because of the wickedness of thy doings, whereby thou hast forsaken me. The LORD shall make the pestilence cleave unto thee, until he have consumed thee from off the land, whither thou goest to possess it. The LORD shall smite thee with a consumption, and with a fever, and with an inflammation, and with an extreme burning, and with the sword, and with blasting, and with mildew; and they shall pursue thee until thou perish. And thy heaven that is over thy head shall be brass, and the earth that is under thee shall be iron. The LORD shall make the rain of thy land powder and dust: from heaven shall it come down upon thee, until thou be destroyed. The LORD shall cause thee to be smitten before thine enemies: thou shalt go out one way against them, and flee seven ways before them: and shalt be removed into all the kingdoms of the earth. And thy carcase shall be meat unto all fowls of the air, and unto the beasts of the earth, and no man shall fray them away. The LORD will smite thee with the botch of Egypt, and with the emerods, and with the scab, and with the itch, whereof thou canst not be healed. The LORD shall smite thee with madness, and blindness, and astonishment of heart: And thou shalt grope at noonday, as the blind gropeth in darkness, and thou shalt not prosper in thy ways: and thou shalt be only oppressed and spoiled evermore, and no man shall save thee. Thou shalt betroth a wife, and another man shall lie with her: thou shalt build an house, and thou shalt not dwell therein: thou shalt plant a vineyard, and shalt not gather the grapes thereof. Thine ox shall be slain before thine eyes, and thou shalt not eat thereof: thine ass shall be violently taken away from before thy face, and shall not be restored to thee: thy sheep shall be given unto thine enemies, and thou shalt have none to rescue them. Thy sons and thy daughters shall be given unto another people, and thine eyes shall look, and fail with longing for them all the day long: and there shall be no might in thine hand. The fruit of thy land, and all thy labours, shall a nation which thou knowest not eat up; and thou shalt be only oppressed and crushed alway: So that thou shalt be mad for the sight of thine eyes which thou shalt see. The LORD shall smite thee in the knees, and in the legs, with a sore botch that cannot be healed, from the sole of thy foot unto the top of thy head. The LORD shall bring thee, and thy king which thou shalt set over thee, unto a nation which neither thou nor thy fathers have known; and there shalt thou serve other gods, wood and stone. And thou shalt become an astonishment, a proverb, and a byword, among all nations whither the LORD shall lead thee. Thou shalt carry much seed out into the field, and shalt gather but little in; for the locust shall consume it. Thou shalt plant vineyards, and dress them, but shalt neither drink of the wine, nor gather the grapes; for the worms shall eat them. Thou shalt have olive trees throughout all thy coasts, but thou shalt not anoint thyself with the oil; for thine olive shall cast his fruit. Thou shalt beget sons and daughters, but thou shalt not enjoy them; for they shall go into captivity. All thy trees and fruit of thy land shall the locust consume. The stranger that is within thee shall get up above thee very high; and thou shalt come down very low. He shall lend to thee, and thou shalt not lend to him: he shall be the head, and thou shalt be the tail. Moreover all these curses shall come upon thee, and shall pursue thee, and overtake thee, till thou be destroyed; because thou hearkenedst not unto the voice of the LORD thy God, to keep his commandments and his statutes which he commanded thee: And they shall be upon thee for a sign and for a wonder, and upon thy seed for ever. Because thou servedst not the LORD thy God with joyfulness, and with gladness of heart, for the abundance of all things; Therefore shalt thou serve thine enemies which the LORD shall send against thee, in hunger, and in thirst, and in nakedness, and in want of all things: and he shall put a yoke of iron upon thy neck, until he have destroyed thee. The LORD shall bring a nation against thee from far, from the end of the earth, as swift as the eagle flieth; a nation whose tongue thou shalt not understand; A nation of fierce countenance, which shall not regard the person of the old, nor shew favour to the young: And he shall eat the fruit of thy cattle, and the fruit of thy land, until thou be destroyed: which also shall not leave thee either corn, wine, or oil, or the increase of thy kine, or flocks of thy sheep, until he have destroyed thee. And he shall besiege thee in all thy gates, until thy high and fenced walls come down, wherein thou trustedst, throughout all thy land: and he shall besiege thee in all thy gates throughout all thy land, which the LORD thy God hath given thee. And thou shalt eat the fruit of thine own body, the flesh of thy sons and of thy daughters, which the LORD thy God hath given thee, in the siege, and in the straitness, wherewith thine enemies shall distress thee: So that the man that is tender among you, and very delicate, his eye shall be evil toward his brother, and toward the wife of his bosom, and toward the remnant of his children which he shall leave: So that he will not give to any of them of the flesh of his children whom he shall eat: because he hath nothing left him in the siege, and in the straitness, wherewith thine enemies shall distress thee in all thy gates. The tender and delicate woman among you, which would not adventure to set the sole of her foot upon the ground for delicateness and tenderness, her eye shall be evil toward the husband of her bosom, and toward her son, and toward her daughter, And toward her young one that cometh out from between her feet, and toward her children which she shall bear: for she shall eat them for want of all things secretly in the siege and straitness, wherewith thine enemy shall distress thee in thy gates. If thou wilt not observe to do all the words of this law that are written in this book, that thou mayest fear this glorious and fearful name, THE LORD THY GOD; Then the LORD will make thy plagues wonderful, and the plagues of thy seed, even great plagues, and of long continuance, and sore sicknesses, and of long continuance. Moreover he will bring upon thee all the diseases of Egypt, which thou wast afraid of; and they shall cleave unto thee. Also every sickness, and every plague, which is not written in the book of this law, them will the LORD bring upon thee, until thou be destroyed. And ye shall be left few in number, whereas ye were as the stars of heaven for multitude; because thou wouldest not obey the voice of the LORD thy God. And it shall come to pass, that as the

LORD rejoiced over you to do you good, and to multiply you; so the LORD will rejoice over you to destroy you, and to bring you to nought; and ye shall be plucked from off the land whither thou goest to possess it. And the LORD shall scatter thee among all people, from the one end of the earth even unto the other; and there thou shalt serve other gods, which neither thou nor thy fathers have known, even wood and stone. And among these nations shalt thou find no ease, neither shall the sole of thy foot have rest: but the LORD shall give thee there a trembling heart, and failing of eyes, and sorrow of mind: And thy life shall hang in doubt before thee; and thou shalt fear day and night, and shalt have none assurance of thy life: In the morning thou shalt say, Would God it were even! and at even thou shalt say, Would God it were morning! for the fear of thine heart wherewith thou shalt fear, and for the sight of thine eyes which thou shalt see. And the LORD shall bring thee into Egypt again with ships, by the way whereof I spake unto thee, Thou shalt see it no more again: and there ye shall be sold unto your enemies for bondmen and bondwomen, and no man shall buy you."
(Deuteronomy 28:1-68)

The blessings were specified for the children of Israel. The nation was given all that is identified in verses 2-14 with the stipulation that they must be obedient. This obedient requirement is repeated 3-4 times. As a note, these were recited for a nation and not for an individual therefore the lending to many nations and not borrowing would only apply if you are a banking institution. In the 15th through the 68th verse of this exact same chapter we read the calamities if one decided not to be obedient. The choice is up to the group or individual. Take a moment and read all the promises and benefits of the covenant. Everything God said He blessed in verses 1-14 He is cursing and there are 3 times as many curses. Verses 1 through 14 compared to verses 15 through 68; you shall be blessed if you are obedient and you shall be triple cursed if you are not. It isn't natural to prefer the cursing over the blessing but it is brought out in the law. The decision and the outcome belong to you but you have to meet the requirements for the blessing of the covenant.

"Thou shalt truly tithe all the increase of thy seed, that the field bringeth forth year by year. And thou shalt eat before the LORD thy God, in the place which he shall choose to place his name there, the tithe of thy corn, of thy wine, and of thine oil, and the firstlings of thy herds and of thy flocks; that thou mayest learn to fear the LORD thy God always. And if the way be too long for thee, so that thou art not able to carry it; or if the place be too far from thee, which the LORD thy God shall choose to set his name there, when the LORD thy God hath blessed thee: Then shalt thou

turn it into money, and bind up the money in thine hand, and shalt go unto the place which the LORD thy God shall choose: And thou shalt bestow that money for whatsoever thy soul lusteth after, for oxen, or for sheep, or for wine, or for strong drink, or for whatsoever thy soul desireth: and thou shalt eat there before the LORD thy God, and thou shalt rejoice, thou, and thine household," (Deuteronomy 14:22-26)

"Thou mayest not eat within thy gates the tithe of thy corn, or of thy wine, or of thy oil, or the firstlings of thy herds or of thy flock, nor any of thy vows which thou vowest, nor thy freewill offerings, or heave offering of thine hand: 18 But thou must eat them before the LORD thy God in the place which the LORD thy God shall choose, thou, and thy son, and thy daughter, and thy manservant, and thy maidservant, and the Levite that is within thy gates: and thou shalt rejoice before the LORD thy God in all that thou puttest thine hands unto." (Deuteronomy 12:17-18)

The tithe according to the law was required to be given for specific reasons. God gave stipulations on what He wanted to be done with the tithe and where it was to be brought. The first ten percent (10%) of everything that you have been given by God whether it be life (firstlings of the herd) or of the ground (corn, wine, oil) would be brought to the place God chose each year.

The first and second year He commands that He selects a place and everyone would bring their tithe and eat it before the Lord. God also identifies why we do this; so that you will learn to fear the Lord and to reverence Him. The tithe presentation was a feast or celebration. Each year of the first two years the tithe would be brought to the location God chose and it would be consumed before the Lord.

"At the end of three years thou shalt bring forth all the tithe of thine increase the same year, and shalt lay it up within thy gates: And the Levite, (because he hath no part nor inheritance with thee,) and the stranger, and the fatherless, and the widow, which are within thy gates, shall come, and shall eat and be satisfied; that the LORD thy God may bless thee in all the work of thine hand which thou doest." (Deuteronomy 14:28-29)

The first two years the people who produced it consumed the tithe as a feast or celebration, that third year it was for the Levite. The Levites were those that were working in the Tabernacle. Looking back at what was given to the twelve (12) tribes as an inheritance the Levites weren't given an inheritance. They were supposed to work within the tabernacle and God was their portion. He was to make sure He took care of them. God declares the place, decides when and the people are to bring the tithe. In the third year instead of a celebration consuming what was brought; it was for the Levite, the stranger, the widow and the fatherless. In God's economy He makes provision for everyone. God invites them to the place and time for a celebration the first two years. In year three the invitation goes out but this time it is a contribution to take care of those who are serving and those who need service. If the distance to the selected location was too far they were allowed to change the animals and vegetation into money. When they got to the location they would purchase what was needed. God through His set up instituted a system that would provide for His economy.

Now moving to the post-exilic period, after exile, Malachi 3:8 *"Will a man rob God? Yet ye have robbed me. But ye say, Wherein have we robbed thee? In tithes and offerings."*

At this juncture the Lord of hosts declares that they were guilty of robbing Him if they did not give tithe and offerings. Let's detail what was identified to give according to the law:

> *"But unto the place which the LORD your God shall choose out of all your tribes to put his name there, even unto his habitation shall ye seek, and thither thou shalt come: And thither ye shall bring your <u>burnt offerings, and your sacrifices, and your tithes, and heave offerings of your hand, and your vows, and your freewill offerings, and the firstlings of your herds and of your flocks</u>: And there ye shall eat before the LORD your God, and ye*

shall rejoice in all that ye put your hand unto, ye and your households, wherein the LORD thy God hath blessed thee."
(Deuteronomy 12:5-7, emphasis mine)

"All the firstling males that come of thy herd and of thy flock thou shalt sanctify unto the LORD thy God: thou shalt do no work with the firstling of thy bullock, nor shear the firstling of thy sheep. Thou shalt eat it before the LORD thy God year by year in the place which the LORD shall choose, thou and thy household. And if there be any blemish therein, as if it be lame, or blind, or have any ill blemish, thou shalt not sacrifice it unto the LORD thy God. Thou shalt eat it within thy gates: the unclean and the clean person shall eat it alike, as the roebuck, and as the hart. Only thou shalt not eat the blood thereof; thou shalt pour it upon the ground as water."
(Deuteronomy 15:19-23)

There are a myriad of offerings referenced in the law each with different percentages attached. Many others can be found in Exodus and Leviticus. Let's summarize what is required:

Tithe 10%
Firstlings 10%
First fruits 1%
1/7th land boundary 14%
feasts and celebrations 5%

sin offering 5%
burnt offerings
sacrifices
heave offering
vows
freewill offerings (given as often as you like during celebration time without limit)

In the Torah, the first five books of the Bible (Genesis, Exodus, Leviticus, Numbers and Deuteronomy) many offerings are listed. They include: burnt offerings; grain offering; peace offering; offerings for sin; trespass offering; offerings for restitution; and offerings for various feasts (Sabbath, Passover, First fruits, Weeks, Trumpets, Atonement, Tabernacle). Now if you were to go back to the law and give your tithe and all the offerings identified it would amount to approximately forty-five percent (~45%) or more of your income. Is that a problem?

Depending on your tax bracket, twenty-five to forty percent (25-40%) of your income goes to Uncle Sam in taxes. If we look back we identified who gives life and everything that pertains to life. We know who gives us the breath that we have and the strength to go on our jobs. So, if God withdrew any of that, where would we be? If He took our mind away so that we would not be able to operate in the field in which we earn our livelihood we would be unable to give to anyone else let alone support ourselves. Proverbs 3 reminds us to honor the Lord with our substance and with the first of our increase. That increase is whatever He's allowed you to obtain. Originally the Bible says to give the first of the animals and they should be without spot or blemish. It's an admonishing to give God the best of the best because we're honoring Him in what we are doing.

The first two years under the law you were eating; you were partaking; you would reverence who He is. You could say, "Thank you Lord that we are partaking of this but we recognize that we are only sharing in this celebration because You have blessed us in such a way that You opened up the windows of heaven". The reference to opening up the windows of heaven in the Old Testament meant that the rain came down to water the crops. The rain was significant because they were an agricultural society. The first fruits in an agricultural society; the first of a crop harvested, or a new business, or a new venture, or a new land development, was given to the Lord. Unless you are a farmer or a business owner you don't have a first fruit offering.

First fruits when you look it up in Hebrew is word *bikkor*. It is the first of the crops and the fruit that ripen and was gathered and offered to God at Pentecost. The bread also made of the new grain was offered. The word first, *ray-sheeth*, meaning beginning, best, chief, who is the choice part in Hebrew and then in the Greek.

First fruit is not giving the first months' salary every year in January. If you are a business owner then the

> **FIRST FRUITS**
> 1061 בִּכּוּרִים [bikkuwr /bik·koor/]
> 1 first-fruits. 1a the first of the crops and fruit that ripened, was gathered, and offered to God according to the ritual of Pentecost. 1b the bread made of the new grain offered at Pentecost. 1c the day of the first-fruits (Pentecost).
> Strong, J. (1995). <u>Enhanced Strong's Lexicon</u>. Woodside Bible Fellowship.
>
> **FIRST**
> 7225 רֵאשִׁית [re'shiyth /ray·sheeth/]
> 1 first, beginning, best, chief. 1a beginning. 1b first. 1c chief. 1d choice part.
> Strong, J. (1995). <u>Enhanced Strong's Lexicon</u>. Woodside Bible Fellowship.

first year you would give off the top to the Lord; it may be the first profits equaling more than 10%. A new venture God has given you would do the same. It still follows the reverence of the tithe. If you get a raise in January this would not be considered first fruit because you would pay your tithe off the gross. If the gross goes up, whenever it occurs, you would recalculate your tithe at that time. First says you are starting something and because this is the beginning you are honoring God so that He will bless the rest. If you were to return to an agricultural society and you began to work the land planting corn, potatoes, beans, etc. then of that first harvest you would give a portion of that crop to the Lord to express your gratitude. Thankful that God gave the land and the crop but He also opened up the

Not Just Paper

windows of heaven making sure the rain fell, the sun shined on it yielding this harvest; you acknowledge God. That first year you are giving first fruit. The rest of the months following you're bringing in the harvest you are still returning the tithe but you're not giving a first fruit offering. That first year you might decide to give all the profits. Some business owners give one hundred percent (100%) of the profits in the first year. When you start something new the first fruit offering is given during that first year.

With the free will offering you can give whatever you want; God is not limiting that offering. With our offerings we are honoring God and we are learning to revere who God is by thanking and appreciating Him. It is given in appreciation of what He has given and what He has done for you. In the Old Testament there were commands to give for different reasons. The sin offering was given because a sin was committed. In the law, the first male child that was born to a family required a sacrifice offering either two turtle doves or a lamb. There was an offering required depending on the wealth of the family. Regarding the land boundary; 1/7 of the land belonged to God. Today we have sidewalks which represents a portion by the road given to the city even though you paid for all of the property. God put these requirements in place and when the children of Israel did not meet the requirement they were chastised. Not doing what God had told them to do was why they went into captivity. God required that the land rest every seventh year. Babylonian captivity was the result of disobedience which then forced the seventy years to be recouped. Even with the tithe and offerings totaling about 45%; we have to declare He is worthy!!

"And the LORD spake unto Moses, saying, Speak unto the children of Israel, that they bring me an offering: of every man that giveth it willingly with his heart ye shall take my offering. And this is the offering which ye shall take of them; gold, and silver, and brass, And blue, and purple, and scarlet, and fine linen, and goats' hair, And rams' skins dyed red, and badgers' skins, and shittim wood, Oil for the light, spices for anointing oil, and for sweet incense, Onyx stones, and stones to be set in the ephod, and in the breastplate. And let them make me a sanctuary; that I may dwell among them." (Exodus 25:1-8)

God set the principle and the basis for storehouse giving; you are to bring an offering so that God can build His sanctuary. The storehouse giving is to take care of the people that are working in the house of God. It was set up from the very beginning to make sure His house that boar His name and the people who boar His name were provided for in His economy. An economy is an orderly function or organized system that is set up. There is income and spending similar to a budget. It's an organized system similar to the economy we have in the USA. For instance, taxes; we work and get paid (income) and taxes go out (income for the government). The economy doesn't work if you don't have money coming into the government (taxes) because they would have no money to give out. Turning our attention to the church, if in the sanctuary, the place of God where He has placed his people, if money doesn't come in (tithe and offering) it doesn't run. So if the people come in and the people sit: in order to have air conditioning for them to be comfortable; in order for them to have lights on so that they can read the Bible or some who didn't bring their Bibles to get to pick up a Bible; in order for the man of God or the woman of God to stand before the people and be able to preach the word and have the time to put into study; there is a need to give. This giving can't just be $1 in the offering plate or a tap. God's economy is designed in such a way that at the place that He chooses He can take care of His house and His people as well as those strangers that are coming in that are in need; there must be income in the storehouse.

> *"And the LORD spake unto Aaron, Thou shalt have no inheritance in their land, neither shalt thou have any part among them: I am thy part and thine inheritance among the children of Israel. And, behold, I have given the children of Levi all the tenth in Israel for an inheritance, for their service which they serve, even the service of the tabernacle of the congregation." (Numbers 18:20,21)*

God is the portion for those who serve Him. If you are a minister or serve in the Kingdom in full time or part time ministry, your rewards are from God and He declares that an inheritance is due you. Your rewards are out of this world but you need income to live in this world until you get there. Relooking at Genesis 15 with Abram, God said He was the supply and would provide. He does this by the economy He set in place. God says, 'I am your exceeding great reward, your increase in the money supply, I will take care of you.' He is doing this with what is being given and taken into the storehouse (local church). This allows the minister or servant to not have to look for a job because we won't contribute to pay them for their service of the Lord. That's not God's economy. When someone serves, whatever they're doing in the Tabernacle, they should be compensated because they're giving themselves wholly to God to do the work that He is asking them to do. God said to the servants (Levites in the Old Testament) I'm not giving you an inheritance, I am not giving you an outside income, I'm not giving you a land boundary like I did with the other tribes, I'm giving you the work in the temple and because you're working in this temple I'm going to compensate you by having others bring a tenth and it's your inheritance.

"At that time the LORD separated the tribe of Levi, to bear the ark of the covenant of the LORD, to stand before the LORD to minister unto him, and to bless in his name, unto this day. Wherefore Levi hath no part nor inheritance with his brethren; the LORD is his inheritance, according as the LORD thy God promised him." (Deuteronomy 10:8,9)

God declared He would be their inheritance because they were different from the rest of the people. They were called to holy service so the Lord possessed both the congregation of Israel and those appointed to serve in the temple of God. The payment (or return) of the tithe was the recognition of the fact that God owned them and all that they possessed. To withhold the tithe was to denounce the Supreme and permanent authority of God in their lives and thus rob God of that which rightfully belongs to Him; which was used for the upkeep of His economy.

The Grace of the Tithe

GRACE
- unmerited favor;
- God's influence on the heart of man and its reflection in one's life.

The grace of the tithe will be found under Jesus Christ. We studied the principle of the tithe under Abraham prior to any law being given. We had the law of the tithe under Moses with the stipulations God laid out to serve His economy. When Jesus comes on the scene He ministers under the law of Moses and he operates under that law until He fulfills all of the law on the cross. So, while Jesus was here on earth, everyone was still under the law for returning the tithe and sacrifices.

"When he was come down from the mountain, great multitudes followed him. And, behold, there came a leper and worshipped him, saying, Lord, if thou wilt, thou canst make me clean. And Jesus put forth his hand, and touched him, saying, I will; be thou clean. And immediately his leprosy was cleansed. And Jesus saith unto him, See thou tell no man; but go thy way, shew thyself to the priest, and offer the gift that Moses commanded, for a testimony unto them." (Matthew 8:1-4)

Jesus commanded the former leper to follow and obey the law. He complied with the law of Moses which was the Torah not the Jewish tradition (Talmud). The Jewish tradition is the written form of the oral complete law.

"Woe unto you, scribes and Pharisees, hypocrites! for ye pay tithe of mint and anise and cummin, and have omitted the weightier matters of the law, judgment, mercy, and faith: these ought ye to have done, and not to leave the other undone." (Matthew 23:23)

In looking at Matthew 23 Jesus says to the self-righteous that they should have paid the tithe and anybody else who was owed. He identifies that tithe paying and others were an entry level matter. He identifies that they paid the tithe but omitted the weightier matters. Tithing is a little matter and should be easily done. In Luke 11:42, Jesus repeats the same sentiment, *"But woe unto you, Pharisees! for ye tithe mint and rue and all manner of herbs, and pass over judgment and the love of God: these ought ye to have done, and not to leave the other undone."*

We are to return the tithe (10%) and give an offering as well because it is required for God's economy. We are stewards or house managers and we don't own anything but are grateful for everything. As a steward we have the mindset that we return a portion of what God has given us to manage to continue His economy. After all, it all belongs to Him and we are just following orders.

> *"He that is faithful in that which is least is faithful also in much: and he that is unjust in the least is unjust also in much. If therefore ye have not been faithful in the unrighteous mammon, who will commit to your trust the true riches? And if ye have not been faithful in that which is another man's, who shall give you that which is your own?" (Luke 16:10-12)*

Jesus expounds on the lesser matter of tithing. He records for us a revelation of the heart attitude represented in giving. If with little you are faithful; you will be faithful when given much. He goes on to identify that the true riches aren't the money gains (unrighteous mammon). And He asks the question, Who will commit to your trust the true riches? If you are faithful in the least, in the giving of money you qualify yourself for the true riches. The true riches could include Kingdom assignments, purpose, impact and influence. It would necessarily include those things that God holds dear.

> *"And he spake this parable unto certain which trusted in themselves that they were righteous, and despised others: Two men went up into the temple to pray; the one a Pharisee, and the other a publican. The Pharisee stood and prayed thus with himself, God, I thank thee, that I am not as other men are, extortioners, unjust, adulterers, or even as this publican. I fast twice in the week, I give tithes of all that I possess. And the publican, standing afar off, would not lift up so much as his eyes unto heaven, but smote upon his breast, saying, God be merciful to me a sinner. I tell you, this man went down to his house justified rather than the other: for every one that exalteth himself shall be abased; and he that humbleth himself shall be exalted." (Luke 18:9-14)*

The self-proclaimed righteous Pharisee while petitioning, highlights the fact that he gives tithes. Though he was really only speaking to himself, he identified the law of the tithe requirement. It appears again as a little matter since later Jesus identifies the law kills but the Spirit brings life. How do we expect the provisions of the covenant without meeting the requirements of the same? We ask God to stand by all of His promises just because we want them... We are requesting benefits just because we have breath.

It used to marvel me that many will call the church or ask for a million dollars from a loving God without having relationship with Him. Why would I as a child of God go to my Father on behalf of someone who doesn't want anything to do with Him and ask Him to give them a million dollars? Asking for relationship and a drawing of the soul to fill a God-sized void is greater than monetary gain.

> **"For Christ is the end of the law for righteousness to every one that believeth."** *(Romans 10:4)*

Jesus operated under the law. He instructed others to meet the requirements. He caused us to examine the heart behind the law for the heart of God. Christ enters earth and He fulfills the law accomplishing completely its requirements. It is abolished; rendered null and void. We are no longer under the law but under grace.

> **"Having abolished in his flesh the enmity, even the law of commandments contained in ordinances; for to make in himself of twain one new man, so making peace;"** *(Ephesians 2:15)*

> **"But now in Christ Jesus, you who one were [so] far away, through (by, in) the blood of Christ have been brought near. For He is**

[Himself] our peace (our bond of unity and harmony). He has made us both [Jew and Gentile] one [body], and has broken down (destroyed, abolished) the hostile dividing wall between us, By abolishing in His [own crucified] flesh the enmity [caused by] the Law with its decrees and ordinances [which He annulled]; that He from the two might create in Himself one new man [one new quality of humanity out of the two], so making peace. And [He designed] to reconcile to God both [Jew and Gentile, united] in a single body by means of His cross, thereby killing the mutual enmity and bringing the feud to an end. And He came and preached the glad tidings of peace to you who were afar off and [peace] to those who were near. For it is through Him that we both [whether far off or near] now have an introduction (access)by one [Holy] Spirit to the Father [so that we are able to approach Him]." (Ephesians 2:13-18, AMP)

The law then no longer has any effect. And based on Jesus' sacrifice, we unified into one, annulling the law and its ordinances. He is our peace. He is our unifier and reconciler. As He was hung on the cross taking our place and giving us access to have peace with God, He was made a curse for us. We are thankful that though the law taught us much, we aren't under the law any longer because of Jesus' sacrifice.

"Christ hath redeemed us from the curse of the law, being made a curse for us: for it is written, Cursed is every one that hangeth on a tree:" (Galatians 3:13)

"Now it is evident that no person is justified (declared righteous and brought into right standing with God) through the Law, for the Scripture says, The man in right standing with God [the just, the righteous] shall live by and out of faith and he who through and by faith is declared righteous and in right standing with God shall live. But the Law does not rest on faith [does not require faith, has nothing to do with faith], for it itself says, He who does them [the things prescribed by the Law] shall live by them [not by faith]. Christ purchased our freedom [redeeming us] from the curse (doom) of the Law [and its condemnation] by [Himself] becoming a curse for us, for it is written [in the Scriptures], Cursed is everyone who hangs on a tree (is crucified); To the end that through [their receiving] Christ Jesus, the blessing [promised] to Abraham might come upon the Gentiles, so that we through faith might [all] receive [the realization of] the promise of the [Holy] Spirit." (Galatians 3:11-14, AMP)

So, Jesus provides grace. Grace to receive an eternal home. Grace to be at peace and not be required to be subject to the power of sin. Grace to endure. Grace also to give freely. In the Old Testament under the law there was the tithe and a lot of offerings that were required. Jesus came in and fulfills it completely operating under the law. He then is no longer under the law nor the curse of the law. In the New Testament, under this grace, Paul gives us instructions on giving because God's economy still needs to operate.

"Moreover, brethren, we do you to wit of the grace of God bestowed on the churches of Macedonia; How that in a great trial of affliction the abundance of their joy and their deep poverty abounded unto the riches of their liberality. For to their power, I bear record, yea, and beyond their power they were willing of themselves; Praying us with much intreaty that we would receive the gift, and take upon us the fellowship of the ministering to the saints. And this they did, not as we hoped, but first gave their own selves to the Lord, and unto us by the will of God. Insomuch that we desired Titus, that as he had begun, so he would also finish in you the same grace also. Therefore, as ye abound in every thing, in faith, and utterance, and knowledge, and in all diligence, and in your love to us, see that ye abound in this grace also." (2 Corinthians 8:1-7).

There has been an offering taken up over the past year to assist the saints that were in need in Jerusalem and the time has come for Paul to send somebody to collect the money received. The Macedonian church were in poverty (lack and want) but they gave generously. The grace of giving is the least or little matter. Paul records as you abound in faith, utterance, knowledge, diligence and love to those who serve you should also abound in the grace of giving. As we give ourselves first, our heart changes. As we meet with God and reason with Him, getting on the same page, our hearts are broken with the same things that break His heart. We see the sacrifice and are willing to be used in many ways by Him. Sometimes that using is for resources to carry on His economy and missions.

> *"For which cause also I have been much hindered from coming to you. But now having no more place in these parts, and having a great desire these many years to come unto you; Whensoever I take my journey into Spain, I will come to you: for I trust to see you in my journey, and to be brought on my way thitherward by you, if first I be somewhat filled with your company. But now I go unto Jerusalem to minister unto the saints. For it hath pleased them of Macedonia and Achaia to make a certain contribution for the poor saints which are at Jerusalem. It hath pleased them verily; and their debtors they are. For if the Gentiles have been made partakers of their spiritual things, their duty is also to minister unto them in carnal things. When therefore I have performed this, and have*

sealed to them this fruit, I will come by you into Spain." (Romans 15:22-28)

Paul records that he was coming through that region and bringing the contributions to the saints. He brags on the saints in Macedonia and Achaia and their giving. It was possibly listed to encourage others to also get their contribution prepared. He identifies that if you are partakers of the spiritual things you are supposed also give them some of your carnal things (monetary compensation).

"Now concerning the collection for the saints, as I have given order to the churches of Galatia, even so do ye. Upon the first day of the week let every one of you lay by him in store, as God hath prospered him, that there be no gatherings when I come. And when I come, whomsoever ye shall approve by your letters, them will I send to bring your liberality unto Jerusalem. And if it be meet that I go also, they shall go with me." (1 Corinthians 16:1-4)

The Apostle Paul admonishes them to make sure they put aside the offering being taken up early. In other words, don't wait until the last minute and try to collect it when I arrive. We know what happens last minute; usually we give less. Whoever you decide will collect the offering must, but you have a responsibility every week to lay aside what you have planned to give. Don't procrastinate until the last moment because it would be embarrassing since you were to be collecting for a year. Wouldn't you rather sow your seed early and see it blooming early than to wait until the last minute and all you have is the seed? If you just put your seed in the ground today and you compare it to one that was planted a year ago, the later may have a tree developing and the former only has a seed. Plant those seeds weekly and consistently; after all, we ask for daily bread. If we are asking God to bless us every day, and He does, and because My God supplies all my needs according to His riches in glory (Philippians 4:19) and a cattle on a thousand hills belongs to Him (Psalm 50:10); there's nothing that is impossible for Him (Luke 1:37). Weekly you can remind yourself that God is the one that has given you the power to get wealth (Deuteronomy 8:18) and is worthy to be thanked for the blessings. Like all acts of obedience, the word of God and the prompting of the Holy Spirit, the giving of tithes, gifts and offerings must now be done by faith in Christ, not a work of the law. God says in His new pattern of giving the requirement to give remains and His economy should be remembered. Under the law, that third year was given to the Levites and it was given to the poor strangers and the widows. The economy still needs to work, so the collection was for those that would have been taken care of in that third years giving. He asks them and us to give unselfishly and cheerfully. They were to give themselves first. Those that give to you spiritual things, we are to communicate (share with them) of our carnal things (money). When we do this adequately, we are taking care of the inheritance of those that are working in the service of the Lord. 2 Corinthians Chapters 8 and 9 all relate to giving.

The New Testament believer is not under the law but under grace, so why tithe? Abraham tithed and he wasn't under the law (see Genesis 14). Jacob tithed in Genesis 28 and he also was before the law and operated under the principle of the tithe. Tithing was done before the law because it was the principle of giving out of reverence and in appreciation. Honoring God for the blessings and helping others by God's grace is a heart motive of giving that pleases God. As we reminisce on what has been given to us because of the sacrifice of Christ we should stand in awe of all that we have received. Love gives and the God kind of love (*agape*) gives freely and sacrificially. Considering the price paid for our lives, tithing should be the minimum standard of giving under grace. Jesus' view of tithing was that it was a minor or little matter. Justice mercy and faith were the weightier matters.

One should examine their heart is if they don't want to give a tithe. After accepting that Jesus has laid down His life for you, thumbing your nose at the sacrifice and everything that God has done as if you bought yourself and pulled yourself up by your own boot straps is ungrateful. You are not your own; you were bought with a price. When you come to the understanding and you bow at the cross and truly acknowledge Jesus as the one who rescued you; there's appreciation. At this time, you then cry out submitting your life and you see Him as Lord and Master. When Jesus is Lord and Master then you follow what He asks you to do. If He asks you to return the tithe so that His kingdom can continue and the economy will work appropriately, you will do it. You can have the right people in place to help you get to that next level of sanctification and then go from glory to glory; following Jesus you are willing to be obedient. You have surrendered and submitted not only your life but your pocketbook as well. If your wallet isn't submitted then maybe you haven't given your heart fully.

> **STANDARD**
> - The thing used as a measure, norm or model in comparative evaluation

The standard is the thing used as a measure, norm or model in comparative evaluation and is identified as the true unadulterated word of God. Tithing is the minimum standard. It is referenced in both the Old and the New Testaments and even commented on by Jesus Himself. Your heart should be willing to do more than the 10% after considering all that God has done. Your heart may be tested when the offering plate is not passed. Do you still give? If no one says anything about it then is your heart being tested? Giving may be one of the hardest areas for individuals to conquer. It may be difficult initially to release the money; but true knowledge of the fact that you are not my own; you were bought with a price and are God's prized possession, should change your attitude toward money. He ransomed you to redeem you; you belong to Him. God will make happen for you what He promised. He will bless your obedience and open up the windows of heaven to pour you out a blessing you don't have room enough to receive (Malachi 3:10). He will also rebuke the devourer for your sake and not allow your prospering to be as holes in your pocket (Haggai 1:6). The Bible records that you can't serve two masters; you will love one and hate the other (Matthew 6:24; Luke 16:13). You can't serve both God and mammon. You can't trust in God and trust in money at the same time. If your trust really is in God then the money can freely fly out of your hand because you know God will supply (Philippians 4:19). If you are faithful in the little you can be ruler of much (Luke 16:10). In Isaiah we saw how the rain came down from heaven and it provided food and seed (Isaiah 55:10). God takes care of you and also allows a blessing for others. You are blessed to be a blessing (Genesis 12:2). If in the Old Testament they gave approximately 45% of all their increase before Jesus came, what more should we be giving? We have all the promises (Old and New Testament) and then some and we get to go before the throne without a go between (Hebrews 4:16). We have the Holy Spirit to guide us 24 hours a day 7 days a week, what is that worth?

Father, help not only our understanding but help us to give more. Help us to be generous with what we have and open our hands that we show compassion upon those who need compassion. Push us to give to Your body so that the work of the Kingdom can go forward without being hindered. We recognize it costs to be on television, it costs to go and share with those in our own communities. We can't have a bread basket or food to give if we don't have the funds. Help us to give and do it consistently and cheerfully. We thank you in advance for answering.

Covenant
Bible Study
Page 233

Chapter 8: Summarizing – The Children of Israel's Journey

As we summarize all that we have discussed regarding Biblical finances, we can trace the children of Israel through their journey. From Egypt to the promised land metaphorically it can be related to our stewardship and our challenges financially. Let's take the journey.

Journey of Children of Israel

Egypt
POVERTY
Land of Lack
House of Bondage

Below Basic Needs

No Time for God
No Talent for Kingdom
No Treasure (money) given

Non Believer

RED SEA
Baptism Into Body Of Christ

Mount Sinai
Provision
Land of Just Enough

Daily Bread
Needs met

Wilderness

Ephesians 1:15-23
Church service
Heard of gifts
Psalm 37:25
Matthew 6:26
New Believer

JORDAN RIVER
Baptism of the Holy Spirit

Gilgal
PROSPERITY
Worship Site

Reminder of God's Faithfulness
Covenant
Motives tested

Deut 8:18
Eph 3:15-19

Tip God
Know gifts
Church & Bible Study

JERICHO
Wall of Greatest Fear
Excuses
Confrontation

Tithe
Infinite steadfast Quality of God's Word

Canaan
Abundance
Land of Plenty
Wealth
Joy of Giving

Prov 3:9-10
Prov 19:17
2 Cor 9:7
Isaiah 55:10
Eph 3:20-21

Devotion +
Grace Giving
Using gifts

Spiritual

The children of Israel were in Egypt and considered to be in poverty which is metaphorically non-believers. We consider them without a real relationship with God; spiritually dead. They were in bondage having to make bricks without straw (Exodus 5:7-18). This is the land of bondage or the land of lack. Our definition of poverty is below our basic needs. We can say that they did not have all of their needs because of the bondage. Here as we look at stewardship relating to time, talents and treasures; there is no time given to God, there is no clue about their talents or gifts and they aren't used in the kingdom and no money is given. That's poverty; living below the basic needs, not having enough and nothing to give to the Lord.

The children of Israel cross the Red Sea on their way to worship God at Mt. Sinai. Crossing over represents their baptism into the body of Christ. At this juncture they've seen a miracle God did for them. They sang and danced because the all-powerful, wonderful, God of the universe took care of their enemies. He provided protection and they acknowledge that. They are now new believers. God brings them out to test them to prove them (Deuteronomy 8:2). He gives them provision by way of daily bread while they are in the wilderness. Manna comes down from heaven each and every day (Exodus 16:15-35). This is the land of just enough. Bread is going to be equivalent to our word of God. Jesus says, "*I am the bread that comes down from heaven*" (John 6:51). Psalm 37:25, David said, *"I was young and now I'm old but I've never seen the righteous forsaken nor his seed begging bread".* Just enough is given; daily bread. In Matthew 6, the model prayer indicates the request to give us this day our daily bread (Matthew 6:11). In Ephesians 1:15-23, Paul prays that the recognition of what we have in Christ is a realization. Why? because they are new believers; just coming into the faith. At this level, one is just figuring out what they are supposed to be doing. As it relates to stewardship, the new believer is coming to church service on Sunday but may not be coming to Bible Study. They know that there are some gifts (spiritual and natural) but are not sure what theirs are. And as far as treasures are concerned they might be tipping God. They are not tithing yet that will come a little later; until the tithe is given all else is a tip.

The children of Israel then cross the Jordan river. The leaders stepped in the river first and they had to select 12 stones from the middle of the river (Joshua 4). The stones were a memorial and set up both in the middle of the river and at the embankment for them to remember what miracle God had done. Every night they would recall at Gilgal the works of God - which became their worship site. The stones were a representation of God's infinite steadfast quality of His word. Their motives were also tested; circumcision comes into play with the covenant of the heart (Deuteronomy 10:16; 30:6; Jeremiah 4:4; Romans 2:29). Written on the table of their hearts, not just tablets of stone now God's word was internalized. Deuteronomy 8:18 records, "**God gives us the power** *to get wealth"*. Paul prays in Ephesians 3:15–29, *"My God is able to do exceeding abundantly above all we could hope, ask or think according to the power that works in us"*. One at this stage might participate in Bible Study adding to their church service. The serving may have increased in relation to time given to God. One is aware of the spiritual gifts, it doesn't mean they are completely walking in it and not consistent. One at this stage may be tipping God a little bit more but not yet tithing.

Tithing comes after the destruction of the Jericho wall. The wall that has to come tumbling down where we finally get the point and recognize that God says return the tithe. Yes, He gave you the power to get wealth but you haven't quite put Him first. The Bible tells us to honor God with our abundance, our increase; He gets the first of everything (Proverbs 3:9). Jericho represents the wall of our greatest fears and our excuses. Those may consist of comments like: "Oh I can't tithe because I can't fit it in my budget"; "I'm afraid I won't have enough money if I try to do this". It's a wall of confrontation because we have to answer the question, Do I really trust God? Am I going to trust Him with everything, including finances? It's a wall that stands just beyond the provision level of prosperity on the way to abundance. When you get pass that Jericho wall you are in the land of Canaan.

Canaan, the land of abundance, is the land of plenty. Every event after Egypt and prior to this is prosperity because you have more than your basic needs. The desire is to be in Canaan, the land of plenty where there's the joy of giving and trusting God. There's a measure above your basic needs out of which you do give to God; you are giving Him something all along the way but by this time you are tithing and giving offerings. You are participating on a regular basis. How do you get from the land of lack into prosperity? You believe. You pray. You bind. You receive. The road the children of Israel traveled relates well to the discussion of Biblical finances.

Business

This same chart can be used as an analogy for other areas in life. We can use it for business as a stewardship example. You start out working for somebody else, you have no time, no money to start a business or whatever God's desire is for you to do. When you cross over the Red Sea and go into Mt. Sinai it could represent you beginning to sell cookies yet you're in somebody else's shop. You might have a small room in a place that you are renting. There's no permanent location, you are not open on a regular basis. You are just covering your expenses, there's no savings. When you get to Gilgal you've crossed the Jordan river; you might have a strip mall location. You are paying rent. You are saving a little. You are giving some back. You are open regularly. At Jericho you have a larger location. The excuse wall comes down and you tithe on your increase. You see your business flourish. You begin investing in your business. Once you pass Jericho, you go on to Canaan. You have a major mall of stores; several locations. It's your shop. You can lease to others and make money from them to pay for your mortgage. You are saving a lot. You are giving a lot and you are investing a lot.

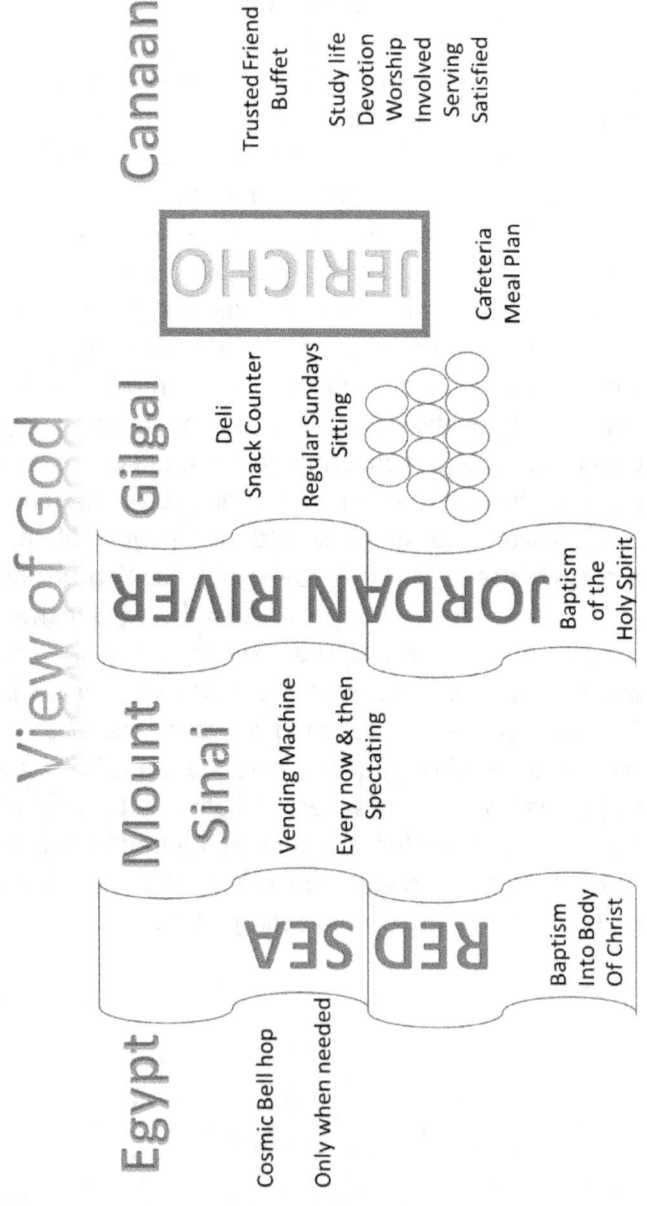

View of God

What is the view of God in these different locations? In Egypt, God is a cosmic bellhop; you only call Him when you need Him. Isn't that what non-believers do? Prayer is requested in dire need and there is the expectation that the lamp is rubbed and the wish is granted but there is no relationship. In Sinai, He's a vending machine; every now and then there is a request. On Sunday, you put a prayer in and get an answer out; you are a spectator. In Gilgal, He's a deli, a snack counter; regularly attending on Sunday and Wednesday. You might be sitting and not serving. It's not just a vending machine on the wall you actually go in the shop and sit down awhile. You may have identified gifts but you aren't working in the shop. At the wall of Jericho, He's a cafeteria meal plan. There is a selected time to visit and it's done on a regular basis. By the time you get to Canaan, He's a trusted friend, a buffet - all you can eat. Grace abundantly flows in your life and you bless others. Your study life is great, your devotion is wonderful and your worship is on point. You're involved, you're serving and satisfied.

Motivation

Egypt — Pain and Want

RED SEA — Baptism Into Body Of Christ

Mount Sinai — Fatigue; Around same mountain

JORDAN RIVER — Baptism of the Holy Spirit

Gilgal — Watching, Trusting, Meditating

JERICHO — Trust/Faith By Experience; Must be Challenged Encouraged

Canaan — Love, Encouraging Others

Motivation

In relation to your motivation: In Egypt it's pain and want and the pain is born out of want. In Sinai, you might be fatigued. You are tired because you're going around that same old mountain over and over again; you haven't quite figured out the relationship. At Gilgal, you have relationship. You trust God and remember His miraculous works. You are building your faith; meditating on His word. Watching other believers is your number one past time. In Jericho, you're trusting; you've got faith backed by experience but you must be challenged and encouraged. By the time you get to Canaan your motivation is nothing but love and you are encouraging other people.

Where are you?

Summarizing the Journey
Bible Study
Page 234

Chapter 9: New Testament Church Giving

So now that Jesus has abolished the law and we are under grace, what type of giving is required? You are now abundantly aware of the earlier requirements - the tithe and offerings. Previously in the first 2 years the tithe was consumed in celebration before the Lord where God chose the place. The third year the tithe was for others, the widows, the orphans, the strangers, and the servants in the house; it was for everyone. That's the pattern laid out in the Old Testament. Now tithe and offering in the New Testament is still going to be part of God's economy and it is needed to support the management of God's Kingdom just like it did in the Old Testament. God is glorified and honored when we give; the receiver glorifies God and God gives a return blessing to the giver. We do and receive this because we are God's representatives; His responsible priesthood. As we work in the Kingdom, God rewards, provides for the workers and receives our sacrifice; His economy continues as we give.

"Am I not an apostle? am I not free? have I not seen Jesus Christ our Lord? are not ye my work in the Lord? If I be not an apostle unto others, yet doubtless I am to you: for the seal of mine apostleship are ye in the Lord. Mine answer to them that do examine me is this, Have we not power to eat and to drink? Have we not power to lead about a sister, a wife, as well as other apostles, and as the brethren of the Lord, and Cephas? Or I only and Barnabas, have not we power to forbear working? Who goeth a warfare any time at his own charges? who planteth a vineyard, and eateth not of the fruit thereof? or who feedeth a flock, and eateth not of the milk of the flock? Say I these things as a man? or saith not the law the same also? For it is written in the law of Moses, Thou shalt not muzzle the mouth of the ox that treadeth out the corn. Doth God take care for oxen? Or saith he it altogether for our sakes? For our sakes, no doubt, this is written: that he that ploweth should plow in hope; and that he that thresheth in hope should be partaker of his hope. If we have sown unto you spiritual things, is it a great thing if we shall reap your carnal things? If others be partakers of this power over you, are not we rather? Nevertheless we have not used this power; but suffer all things, lest we should hinder the gospel of Christ." (1 Corinthians 9:1-12)

Do we send soldiers to war and ask them to pay for their own equipment and travel? Do we ask one to be a farmer and not have food for their own family? Then it should naturally follow that we don't require one to serve us a spiritual meal for free.

"... do not muzzle the ox that treadeth out the corn." (verse 9)

The oxen in the Old Testament were usually yoked together and corn was placed on the ground in front of them as they were plowing. They would see the corn and would want to eat it which would keep them moving forward. You are not supposed to muzzle the ox by putting a brace or contraption on their mouth that prevents them from eating while making them work. An analogy we can relate to would be going to work every day and not getting paid on payday. It would be inappropriate for one to work all week and on payday the building is empty. If you work, you expect to be paid. When the ox is put to work plowing it is expected that he will have the ability to eat the corn laid out in front of him. Don't hinder or muzzle the ox (Deuteronomy 25:4). That is unfair and that is what is referenced in the passage also relating to how we treat servants of the living God.

"... he that ploweth should plow in hope..." (verse 10)

There should be an expectation of something good when you plow. You expect to be a partaker. Just as the expectation is of one who labors to receive payment, so is the request of the servant.

"If we have sown unto you spiritual things, is it a great thing if we shall reap your carnal things?" (verse 11)

Those that sow into you spiritual things should reap of your carnal things. Looking at the natural you should now understand the spiritual. If others have labored in the word and in doctrine and given to you so that you have the practical application, so that your relationship with the heavenly father is now even better and you're getting answers to your prayers, then don't just acknowledge they worked hard. Don't muzzle them by not giving them any monetary compensation for their labor.

"If others be partakers of this power over you, are not we rather? Nevertheless we have not used this power; but suffer all things, lest we should hinder the gospel of Christ."
(1 Corinthians 9:12)

Paul was a tent maker by trade and he ministered to the people. He worked instead of asking the people to provide for him and his co-labourers. They would have meetings for a week and the people wouldn't want to provide for them. Though they sowed into them the spiritual things, they didn't want to be a burden to the gospel. Paul lets them know it is appropriate for them to request according to verse 13. *"Do ye not know that they which minister about holy things live of the things of the temple? and they which wait at the altar are partakers with the altar?"* Remember the Levites serving in the temple; God is their inheritance. God is their money supply and He takes care of them through the economy system He set up. Those that preach the gospel should have a living provided for by those who receive.

"But I have used none of these things: neither have I written these things, that it should be so done unto me: for it were better for me to die, than that any man should make my glorying void." *(verse 15)*

The Apostle Paul refers to the financial support for God's leaders that serve His temple. Man does not go to war at his own expense; a farmer does not reap a harvest yet suffer from starvation. A feeder or shepherd does not feed the flock (his congregation) and not partake of its increase. Just like you take care of your animals that are working in your vineyard or working in your field you're going to take care of those who are working in His field. The one that has been appointed to plant the spiritual riches of the kingdom of God into the life of the believer in Christ has a right to partake of their material increase for physical life on this earth. We don't expect our ministers to do their clerical duties on the side. We don't want them to haphazardly minister to us the word of God. We don't want a Saturday night special because it kills both them and us; we don't want them staying up until 5 am and then getting 1 hour of sleep before ministering to us. They need enough time to study to get all that God has for them to pour out. We can't have it both ways asking them for full time ministry but requiring they also have a full time job. The request isn't biblical. We don't send them to war or have them farm and expect them to pay for it or not eat; it is illogical. God specifies it. Some come into the local assembly assuming they don't have a responsibility to take care of the man or woman of God that are giving their lives in order that their spiritual life might flourish. God's chosen vessels or those who serve in leadership in the church should be given consideration when it comes to sharing in the body's material increase.

"Let the elders that rule well be counted worthy of double honour, especially they who labour in the word and doctrine. For the scripture saith, Thou shalt not muzzle the ox that treadeth out the corn. And, The labourer is worthy of his reward." (1 Timothy 5:17-18)

An elder is a mature individual with character and the ability to teach. Paul as he sets Timothy and Titus, had them appoint elders in different locations. These mature saints were believers able to assist. Sometimes the word pastor and elder are synonymous, this case is one of them. The elder that is ruling well (leading well) is worthy of double honor (verse 17). Double honor is translated from two Greek words which referred to financial remuneration or compensation so that they could fulfill their ministerial duties. That doesn't mean that we give them a double hand clap of praise or put together a video presentation for their twentieth year. Double honor says that they should reap a financial reward. If they are not ruling well they shouldn't be in position; that's not consideration for this topic.

> *"And you Philippians yourselves well known that in the early days of the Gospel ministry, when I left Macedonia, no church (assembly) entered into partnership with me and opened up [a debit and credit] account in giving and receiving except you only. For even in Thessalonica you sent [me contributions] for my needs, not only once but a second time. Not that I seek or am eager for [your] gift, but I do seek and am eager for the fruit which increases to your credit [the harvest of blessing that is accumulating to your account]. But I have [your full payment] and more; I have everything I need and am amply supplied, now that I have received from Epaphroditus the gifts you sent me. [They are the] fragrant odor of an offering and sacrifice which God welcomes and in which He delights. And my God will liberally supply (fill to the full) your every need according to His riches in glory in Christ Jesus. To our God and Father be glory forever and ever (through the endless eternities of the eternities). Amen (so be it)." (Philippians 4:15-20, AMP)*

Paul relates that it's not that he was in need or was eager for them to give to him but he was eager for them to have the fruit that increases to their credit. When you give into God's kingdom it's for your benefit. The harvest is accumulating to your account so when you make a prayer request you have something available to take out and it will not come back insufficient funds. In Philippians 4, Paul talks about generosity being rewarded.

"But godliness with contentment is great gain."
(1 Timothy 6:6)

Contentment says that you are auto-sufficient with Christ. Godliness, your character following after God's character with contentment, satisfied with what God has given you is great gain. You will increase more because God will reward.

The Principle of the tithe was initiated by Abraham when the law had not been given. His motivation was out of appreciation. The Law of the tithe was established under Moses. God sets the requirements/covenant and tests the heart of man. Obedience is required for the rewards. The Grace of the tithe was instituted under Jesus. We as new testament believers are in the grace giving dispensation. If God was appreciated for what He was doing in the land during the time of Abraham, Isaac, and Jacob then when Christ died for us, what more should we give? This means tithing should be the minimum standard of giving for us because Jesus gave His entire life. He didn't give just a hand but He gave it all. If He had not given it all, we would not have been able to be engrafted into the body. He didn't remove only a portion of your sin; He took it all. So now if He took all of your sins, He took all of your wants, He is your Shepherd so that you shall not want and you are willing to go to Him for all, then you should be willing to give. All the benefits of the old covenant and all the benefits of the new covenant are ours in this better covenant. If we really consider what we have, why would we hold back? Greed, selfishness, covetousness. We've been washed by the Word because the Word convicts us. We no longer consider it irritating when the request for offering is presented nor verbalize that the church only wants money. When you go out to eat, don't they ask for money? And you gladly give it to them including a 15% tip for the waitress. God only asks for 10%! So, when you come and you dine, and that spiritual meal that is prepared before you is presented as a buffet, you ought to be grateful and willing to give and tip.

God's Purpose for Giving

We give out of obedience to the Word knowing that God will reward our obedience including the area of finances. As God's responsible priesthood there's one reason we give:

> *"But we see Jesus, who was made a little lower than the angels for the suffering of death, crowned with glory and honour; that*

he by the grace of God should taste death for every man." (Hebrews 2:9)

"And again, I will put my trust in him. And again, Behold I and the children which God hath given me. Forasmuch then as the children are partakers of flesh and blood, he also himself likewise took part of the same; that through death he might destroy him that had the power of death, that is, the devil; And deliver them who through fear of death were all their lifetime subject to bondage. For verily he took not on him the nature of angels; but he took on him the seed of Abraham. Wherefore in all things it behoved him to be made like unto his brethren, that he might be a merciful and faithful high priest in things pertaining to God, to make reconciliation for the sins of the people. For in that he himself hath suffered being tempted, he is able to succour them that are tempted." (Hebrews 2:13-18)

"So it is evident that it was essential that He be made like His brethren in every respect, in order that He might become a merciful (sympathetic) and faithful High Priest in the things related to God, to make atonement and propitiation for the people's sins. For because He Himself [in His humanity] has suffered in being tempted (tested and tried), He is able [immediately] to run to the cry of *(assist, relieve) those who are being tempted and tested and tried [and who therefore are being exposed to suffering]." (Hebrews 2:17-18, AMP)*

Jesus is merciful, compassionate and understanding. Faithful, dependable and always there; that's our High Priest.

"We have not a high priest that is unable to feel that the feelings of our infirmities but in all points he was tempted yet without sin." (Hebrews 4:15)

Jesus has a responsible priesthood so He is the High priest of our confession. He knows, He cares, He understands and He's been there. He was tempted but He did not yield to the temptation. Because of that we have an example and an advocate.

"If therefore perfection were by the Levitical priesthood, (for under it the people received the law,) what further need was there that another priest should rise after the order of Melchisedec, and not be called after the order of Aaron?" (Hebrews 7:11)

The Levitical priesthood was not sufficient or perfect which necessitated a change. The Aaronic priesthood (after Aaron) and the Levitical priesthood (descents of tribe of Levi) had to be born through that particular bloodline. Jesus didn't come from that bloodline, He was of the tribe of Judah. Jesus was the perfect sacrifice which could not be offered by the previous priests.

"And it is yet far more evident: for that after the similitude of Melchisedec there ariseth another priest." (Hebrews 7:15)

Jesus' appointment was not after the fleshly commandment but after the power of an endless life. He was made a priest forever after the order of Melchizedek. Moses gave the law but it had been disannulled when Jesus came and fulfilled the law; it is unprofitable. We still keep the commandments but we recognize when Jesus came He said you have heard of old thou shalt not (Matthew 5:21-33). The 10 commandments and the additional 613 that were added are important. It's not just the letter of the law that kills but the spirit that is behind it (2 Corinthians 3:6). As Jesus taught then not only do you not kill but if you are angry with your brother you've already killed him as well because you have killed his dreams (Matthew 5:22). If you look on a woman to lust after her (desire) you've already committed adultery in your heart (Matthew 5:28). It's a heart matter. Matthew Chapters 5,6 & 7 takes the requirements to another level because Jesus had a sinless life and instructs us on how to apply the principles.

"For it is witnessed of Him, You are a Priest forever after the order (with the rank) of Melchizedek. So a previous physical regulation and command is cancelled

because of its weakness and ineffectiveness and uselessness- For the Law never made anything perfect – but instead a better hope is introduced through which we [now] come close to God. And it was not without the taking of an oath [that Christ was made Priest]." (Hebrews 7:17-20, AMP)

God determined the type of priesthood going forward. No birth rite; not one that man tried, but a new priesthood. Jesus is the High Priest of a better covenant.

"By so much was Jesus made a surety of a better testament. And they truly were many priests, because they were not suffered to continue by reason of death: But this man, because he continueth ever, hath an unchangeable priesthood. Wherefore he is able also to save them to the uttermost that come unto God by him, seeing he ever liveth to make intercession for them." (Hebrews 7:22-25)

There is no mess that Jesus cannot save you from; He's able to save to the uttermost. Why? Because He's a priest after a different order. It wasn't because man suggested or selected but it came from the Father's mouth. It's a new priesthood, a new order; the law has been fulfilled and annulled. The law didn't make us perfect, it just showed us how messed up we were (Hebrews 7:19). God's hope (expectation) is even better than that; He makes us perfect. He that has begun a good work is able to perform it, able to complete it (Philippians 1:6). We might not see it on this side but God is able.

"Ye also, as lively stones, are built up a spiritual house, an holy priesthood, to offer up spiritual sacrifices, acceptable to God by Jesus Christ. Wherefore also it is contained in the scripture, Behold, I lay in Sion a chief corner stone, elect, precious: and he that believeth on him shall not be confounded. Unto you therefore which believe he is precious: but unto them which be disobedient, the stone which the builders disallowed, the same is made the head of the corner, And a stone of stumbling, and a rock of offence, even to them which stumble at the word, being disobedient: whereunto also they were appointed. But ye are a chosen generation, a royal priesthood, an holy nation, a peculiar people; that ye should shew forth the praises of him who hath called you out of darkness into his marvellous light: Which in time past were not a people, but are now the people of God: which had not obtained mercy, but now have obtained mercy." (1 Peter 2:5-10)

We are a royal priesthood. A priest speaks to the people on behalf of God and goes before God on behalf of the people. You are that priesthood now.

Jesus is our High Priest; it doesn't matter in which tribe we were born. Most of us weren't born in a Jewish tribe; after the Levitical priesthood. We weren't established as priests from the law yet God made the appointment; it didn't come from man. The word of God indicates that you are supposed to show forth the praises - the accolades, the adoration, the worship - of Him that has called you out of darkness and into His marvelous light (1 Peter 2:9). We are supposed to act like we are chosen, we are redeemed.

"Honour the LORD with thy substance, and with the firstfruits of all thine increase: So shall thy barns be filled with plenty, and thy presses shall burst out with new wine." (Proverbs 3:9,10)

When we give, we're honoring God and we're also glorifying Him. We give in faith, trusting, relying and depending on Him to supply our every need. It's not because of the law that we give.

"But without faith it is impossible to please him: for he that cometh to God must believe that he is, and that he is a rewarder of them that diligently seek him." (Hebrews 11:6)

We believe God is going to reward us as we give by faith. You should not give to get but you know if you give you will be rewarded. There are plenty of Scriptures that validate the reward.

"But is under tutors and governors until the time appointed of the father. Even so we, when we were children, were in bondage under the elements of the world: But when the fulness of the time was come, God sent forth his Son, made of a woman, made under the law, To redeem them that were under the law, that we might receive the adoption of sons. And because ye are sons, God hath sent forth the Spirit of his Son into your hearts, crying, Abba, Father. Wherefore thou art no more a servant, but a son; and if a son, then an heir of God through Christ." (Genesis 4:2-7)

God says if you do well, if you give your best, He will be pleased and will accept and respect your offering. But if you don't, sin is lying at the door. Not showing up at service until the offering is complete shows a fallacy in the heart. God will reward us according to our obedience to His word. It was not because it was a blood offering that God accepted Abel's offering. It was because Abel gave his best; it was his heart motive behind the giving.

"By faith Abel offered unto God a more excellent sacrifice than Cain, by which he obtained witness that he was righteous, God testifying of his gifts: and by it he being dead yet speaketh." (Hebrews 11:4)

He gave by faith. When Abel gave his offering, he was believing God for a reward and offered his best. When he gave it, he didn't short change God. They weren't given the commandment but they were told by their father Adam to give. In the determination of God accepting one and rejecting the other, there was a recognition that God will respect some and may not respect others. We can't tip God. You don't give an offering until after you have met the tithe requirement. Suppose you go to a restaurant and order a meal. The meal comes and you eat it but only leave a tip. That so-called tip would go toward the cost of the meal and you would still be found lacking. Some would like to only give an offering but if you haven't met the tithe you are insufficient in your covenant account. For example: you have an account at a store. You owe x number of dollars and so you pay on it. You are not giving an offering; you are paying on what you are supposed to give. It's given in hope that you meet that requirement before the end of the year; otherwise you're still lacking and the item remains in the store.

"For in Jesus Christ neither circumcision availeth any thing, nor uncircumcision; but faith which worketh by love." (Galatians 5:6)

Circumcision has now become a covenant of the heart. Christ died for us demonstrating His love for us in that while we were yet sinners, He gave all (Romans 5:8). Our trust, our reliance, our dependence upon who He is and what He is able to do is working through our love. You love Him because He first loved you (1 John 4:19); you are responding to that love.

We must give in faith and recognize the gift that is given then glorifies God, it adds weight. It adds substance. When you honor God with your substance, you are recognizing the Deuteronomy 8:18 passage that God is the one that gave you the power to get wealth. You acknowledge His preeminence. As you complete your budget make sure you include the tithe (10%) first. It can also be a witnessing tool if an accountant or if your child asks why you do it. You are acknowledging that if you did not have God in your life, things would be different and you can give your testimony. If you stand firm on the fact that He is able to supply, you can look at past budgets and see that it should not have worked, but God. When you testify to what He has done you are glorifying God; adding weight. God does not need your money; but you need to give because then by faith, He can reward you openly.

God's purpose in giving includes the fact that you are a priest so you're representing Him. You're honoring and glorifying Him in your giving; and the receiver in turn glorifies God as well. Imagine that you bless somebody because God has laid it on your heart to be a generous giver. You see a need and you fill it; they say, "Well praise God!". They acknowledge God because you were the giver. The gift glorifies God because you gave by faith - because you are trusting, relying and depending upon Him and being obedient to His word.

> "When thou hast made an end of tithing all the tithes of thine increase the third year, which is the year of tithing, and hast given it unto the Levite, the stranger, the fatherless, and the widow, that they may eat within thy gates, and be filled; Then thou shalt say before the LORD thy God, I have brought away the hallowed things out of mine house, and also have given them unto the Levite, and unto the stranger, to the fatherless, and to the widow, according to all thy commandments which thou hast commanded me: I have not transgressed thy commandments, neither have I forgotten them: I have not eaten thereof in my mourning, neither have I taken away ought thereof for any unclean use, nor given ought thereof for the dead: but I have hearkened to the voice of the LORD my God, and have done according to all that thou hast commanded me. Look down from thy holy habitation, from heaven, and bless thy people Israel, and the land which thou hast given us, as thou swarest unto our fathers, a land that floweth with milk and honey." (Deuteronomy 26:12-15)

After obedience came blessing and the receiver praises God for the provision.

> "Ye are the salt of the earth: but if the salt have lost his savour, wherewith shall it be salted? it is thenceforth good for nothing, but

> to be cast out, and to be trodden under foot of men. Ye are the light of the world. A city that is set on an hill cannot be hid. Neither do men light a candle, and put it under a bushel, but on a candlestick; and it giveth light unto all that are in the house. Let your light so shine before men, that they may see your good works, and glorify your Father which is in heaven." (Matthew 5:13-16)

Spectators will see your good works and glorify your Father which is in heaven. That is in the subjective tense, it's a possibility that they will. Though it isn't guaranteed because of their heart, it is still a great opportunity to exalt God. You glorify in your good works. The receiver glorifies because of the good works.

> "[Consider this:] What soldier at any time serves at his own expense? Who plants a vineyard and does not eat any of the fruit of it? Who tends a flock and does not partake of the milk of the flock? Do I say this only on human authority and as a man reasons? Does not the Law endorse the same principle? For in the Law of Moses it is written, You shall not muzzle an ox when it is treading out the corn. Is it [only] for oxen that God cares? Or does He speak certainly and entirely for our sakes? [Assuredly] it is written for our sakes, because the plowman out to plow in hope, and the thresher ought to

thresh in expectation of partaking of the harvest. If we have sown [the seed of] spiritual good among you, [is it too] much if we reap from your material benefits? If others share in this rightful claim upon you, do not we [have a still better and greater claim]? However, we have never exercised this right, but we endure everything rather than put a hindrance in the way [of the spread] of the good news (the Gospel) of Christ. Do you not know that those men who are employed in the services of the temple get their food from the temple? And that those who tend the altar share with the altar [in the offerings brought]? [On the same principle] the Lord directed that those who publish the good news (the Gospel) should live (get their maintenance) by the Gospel. But I have not made use of any of these privileges, nor am I writing this [to suggest] that any such provision be made for me [now]. For it would be better for me to die than to have anyone make void and deprive me of my [ground for] glorifying [in this matter]." (1 Corinthians 9:7-15, AMP)

"Let the elders that rule well be counted worthy of double honour, especially they who labour in the word and doctrine. For the scripture saith, Thou shalt not muzzle the ox that treadeth out the corn. And, The labourer is worthy of his reward." (1 Timothy 5:17-18)

Elders are worthy of double honor; and they will also glorify God. The gift, the giver and the receiver all glorify God.

"Let him that is taught in the word communicate unto him that teacheth in all good things." (Galatians 6:6)

We should make sure that we give remuneration or compensation with sharing (*koinonia*) with them for whatsoever a man soweth that shall he also reap (Galatians 6:7). He that sows to the flesh shall of the flesh reap corruption, but he that soweth to the spirit shall of the spirit reap unto life everlasting (Galatians 6:8). When you reap because you didn't faint, you will give God glory. As we then have opportunity, let us do good unto all men especially them of the household of faith (Galatians 6:10).

"He that hath pity upon the poor lendeth unto the LORD; and that which he hath given will he pay him again." (Proverbs 19:17)

When you give to the poor, you lend to the Lord and God will repay. He pays all his debts with extra. In God's giving, we are giving because we are a holy priesthood identified by Him. We are honoring God and giving Him glory. The receiver is also then going to turn around and glorify God. But the giver receives a return as well.

"While the earth remaineth, seedtime and harvest, and cold and heat, and summer and winter, and day and night shall not cease." (Genesis 8:22)

"Be not deceived; God is not mocked: for whatsoever a man soweth, that shall he also reap. For he that soweth to his flesh shall of the flesh reap corruption; but he that soweth to the Spirit shall of the Spirit reap life everlasting. And let us not be weary in well doing: for in due season we shall reap, if we faint not. As we have therefore opportunity, let us do good unto all men, especially unto them who are of the household of faith." (Galatians 6:7-10)

"If anyone fails to provide for his relatives and especially for those of his own family, he has disowned the faith [by failing to accompany it with fruits] and is worse than an unbeliever [who performs his obligation in these matters]." (1 Timothy 5:8, AMP)

As parents we recognize that all of our labor as we give to our children no matter how many times they come back; eventually they are going to be taking care of us. When we raise them right and they follow God's word; the Bible declares a good man leaves an inheritance for his children's children (Proverbs 13:22). We don't leave the full weight of the financial burden on them to bury us and take care of final expenses. They should take care of you, maybe with your own money. That love and that care and that concern you gave is going to come back; you are going to reap what you've put in. They're not going to be worse than an infidel. What you have given will be returned to you. It may be from different avenues; but be not deceived God is not mocked. They are not going to make an open shame of you; keep on sowing.

> *"And he began again to teach by the sea side: and there was gathered unto him a great multitude, so that he entered into a ship, and sat in the sea; and the whole multitude was by the sea on the land. And he taught them many things by parables, and said unto them in his doctrine, Hearken; Behold, there went out a sower to sow: And it came to pass, as he sowed, some fell by the way side, and the fowls of the air came and devoured it up. And some fell on stony ground, where it had not much earth; and immediately it sprang up, because it had no depth of earth: But when the sun was up, it was scorched; and because it had no root, it withered away. And some fell among thorns, and the thorns grew up, and choked it, and it yielded no fruit. And other fell on good ground, and did yield fruit that sprang up and increased; and brought forth, some thirty, and some sixty, and some an hundred. And he said unto them, He that hath ears to hear, let him hear. And when he was alone, they that were about him with the*

twelve asked of him the parable. And he said unto them, Unto you it is given to know the mystery of the kingdom of God: but unto them that are without, all these things are done in parables: That seeing they may see, and not perceive; and hearing they may hear, and not understand; lest at any time they should be converted, and their sins should be forgiven them. And he said unto them, Know ye not this parable? and how then will ye know all parables? The sower soweth the word. And these are they by the way side, where the word is sown; but when they have heard, Satan cometh immediately, and taketh away the word that was sown in their hearts. And these are they likewise which are sown on stony ground; who, when they have heard the word, immediately receive it with gladness; And have no root in themselves, and so endure but for a time: afterward, when affliction or persecution ariseth for the word's sake, immediately they are offended. And these are they which are sown among thorns; such as hear the word, And the cares of this world, and the deceitfulness of riches, and the lusts of other things entering in, choke the word, and it becometh unfruitful. And these are they which are sown on good ground; such as hear the word, and receive it, and bring forth fruit, some thirtyfold, some sixty, and some an hundred." (Mark 4:1-20)

The sower sows the word of God. When the message is preached some only mention the hundred-fold return. However, the return depends heavily on the soil. With a hundred-fold return lives are changed, destiny's altered, people come to salvation, someone applies the message, and others show the fruit in their life. Sometimes there is only a thirty-fold return, no one responds. It may be years down the road when they react; you can't expect that everybody will necessarily receive what has been sown immediately. The Bible says that we're supposed to speak to one another in Psalms, hymns and spiritual songs making melody in our hearts (Ephesians 5:19); we have an opportunity to sow the word every day. It doesn't have to be from a pulpit, it doesn't have to be from a specific class but when you are encouraging another believer you are sowing the word. Sometimes you will receive thirty-fold, sometimes sixty and sometimes one hundred-fold return. If you give mercy, you're going to receive mercy. If you sow compassion, you will reap compassion. Whatever you sow that shall you also reap.

Genesis 26:8-12 adds to our discussion showing a one hundredfold return, *"And it came to pass, when he had been there a long time, that Abimelech king of the Philistines looked out at a window, and saw, and, behold, Isaac was sporting with Rebekah his wife. And Abimelech called Isaac, and said, Behold, of a surety she is thy wife: and how saidst thou, She is my sister? And Isaac said unto him, Because I said, Lest I die for her. And Abimelech said, What is this thou hast done unto us? one of* the people might lightly have lien with thy wife, and thou shouldest have brought guiltiness upon us. And Abimelech charged all his people, saying, He that toucheth this man or his wife shall surely be put to death. Then Isaac sowed in that land, and received in the same year an hundredfold: and the LORD blessed him."

"And when he was gone forth into the way, there came one running, and kneeled to him, and asked him, Good Master, what shall I do that I may inherit eternal life? And Jesus said unto him, Why callest thou me good? there is none good but one, that is, God. Thou knowest the commandments, Do not commit adultery, Do not kill, Do not steal, Do not bear false witness, Defraud not, Honour thy father and mother. And he answered and said unto him, Master, all these have I observed from my youth. Then Jesus beholding him loved him, and said unto him, One thing thou lackest: go thy way, sell whatsoever thou hast, and give to the poor, and thou shalt have treasure in heaven: and come, take up the cross, and follow me. And he was sad at that saying, and went away grieved: for he had great possessions. And Jesus looked round about, and saith unto his disciples, How hardly shall they that have riches enter into the kingdom of God! And the disciples were astonished at his words. But Jesus answereth again, and saith unto them,

Children, how hard is it for them that trust in riches to enter into the kingdom of God! It is easier for a camel to go through the eye of a needle, than for a rich man to enter into the kingdom of God. And they were astonished out of measure, saying among themselves, Who then can be saved? And Jesus looking upon them saith, With men it is impossible, but not with God: for with God all things are possible. Then Peter began to say unto him, Lo, we have left all, and have followed thee. And Jesus answered and said, Verily I say unto you, There is no man that hath left house, or brethren, or sisters, or father, or mother, or wife, or children, or lands, for my sake, and the gospel's, But he shall receive an hundredfold now in this time, houses, and brethren, and sisters, and mothers, and children, and lands, with persecutions; and in the world to come eternal life. But many that are first shall be last; and the last first." (Mark 10:17-31)

Considering what has been given up Jesus identifies that we shall receive a hundred-fold now and in the world to come eternal life. Now that's more than a hundred-fold return. When we sow we do so bountifully because He promised a return; we can put a praise on it even before the manifestation.

God's Miracle Provision Reminders:

"Now unto him that is able to do exceeding abundantly above all that we ask or think, according to the power that worketh in us." (Ephesians 3:20)

"A good man leaveth an inheritance to his children's children: and the wealth of the sinner is laid up for the just." (Proverbs 13:22)

"Now there cried a certain woman of the wives of the sons of the prophets unto Elisha, saying, Thy servant my husband is dead; and thou knowest that thy servant did fear the LORD: and the creditor is come to take unto him my two sons to be bondmen. And Elisha said unto her, What shall I do for thee? tell me, what hast thou in the house? And she said, Thine handmaid hath not any thing in the house, save a pot of oil. Then he said, Go, borrow thee vessels abroad of all thy neighbours, even empty vessels; borrow not a few. And when thou art come in, thou shalt shut the door upon thee and upon thy sons, and shalt pour out into all those vessels, and thou shalt set aside that which is full. So she went from him, and shut the door upon her and upon her sons, who brought the vessels to her; and she poured out. And it came to pass, when the vessels were full, that she

said unto her son, Bring me yet a vessel. And he said unto her, There is not a vessel more. And the oil stayed. Then she came and told the man of God. And he said, Go, sell the oil, and pay thy debt, and live thou and thy children of the rest." (2 Kings 4:1-7)

"And when they were come to Capernaum, they that received tribute money came to Peter, and said, Doth not your master pay tribute? He saith, Yes. And when he was come into the house, Jesus prevented him, saying, What thinkest thou, Simon? of whom do the kings of the earth take custom or tribute? of their own children, or of strangers? Peter saith unto him, Of strangers. Jesus saith unto him, Then are the children free. Notwithstanding, lest we should offend them, go thou to the sea, and cast an hook, and take up the fish that first cometh up; and when thou hast opened his mouth, thou shalt find a piece of money: that take, and give unto them for me and thee." (Matthew 17:24-27)

"And Elijah the Tishbite, who was of the inhabitants of Gilead, said unto Ahab, As the LORD God of Israel liveth, before whom I stand, there shall not be dew nor rain these years, but according to my word. And the word of the LORD came unto him, saying, Get thee hence, and turn thee eastward, and

hide thyself by the brook Cherith, that is before Jordan. And it shall be, that thou shalt drink of the brook; and I have commanded the ravens to feed thee there. So he went and did according unto the word of the LORD: for he went and dwelt by the brook Cherith, that is before Jordan. And the ravens brought him bread and flesh in the morning, and bread and flesh in the evening; and he drank of the brook. And it came to pass after a while, that the brook dried up, because there had been no rain in the land. And the word of the LORD came unto him, saying, Arise, get thee to Zarephath, which belongeth to Zidon, and dwell there: behold, I have commanded a widow woman there to sustain thee. So he arose and went to Zarephath. And when he came to the gate of the city, behold, the widow woman was there gathering of sticks: and he called to her, and said, Fetch me, I pray thee, a little water in a vessel, that I may drink. And as she was going to fetch it, he called to her, and said, Bring me, I pray thee, a morsel of bread in thine hand. And she said, As the LORD thy God liveth, I have not a cake, but an handful of meal in a barrel, and a little oil in a cruse: and, behold, I am gathering two sticks, that I may go in and dress it for me and my son, that we may eat it, and die. And Elijah said unto her, Fear not; go and do as thou hast said: but make me thereof a little cake first, and bring it unto me, *and after make for thee and for thy son. For thus saith the LORD God of Israel, The barrel of meal shall not waste, neither shall the cruse of oil fail, until the day that the LORD sendeth rain upon the earth. And she went and did according to the saying of Elijah: and she, and he, and her house, did eat many days. And the barrel of meal wasted not, neither did the cruse of oil fail, according to the word of the LORD, which he spake by Elijah." (1 Kings 17:1-16)*

In 1 Kings 17, we have the account of Elijah when he left Gilead and went by the brook Cherith and was feed by ravens. A dirty bird fed him quail on toast in the morning and quail on toast in the evening. Elijah declared there would not be any rain and the brook was drying up. Elijah was sent to the widow after God had miraculously provided through a bird. The widow acknowledged she had only a little for the last meal for her son and herself before they would die. The prophet requested a cake for himself first. Because she did what was asked she never ran out of oil. The prophet Elisha had some of the same miraculous events occur. Twice as many miracles are recorded because he asked for a double portion (2 Kings 2:9). There was a widow that came to Elisha also with an oil issue; debtors were coming to collect after her husband died (2 Kings 4:1-7). She kept pouring oil until the vessels ran out.

Miraculous events still occur today when we believe. Meditating on what was done in the past will build our faith for our current situation. Consider these events. Jesus as he was on the water said cast your nets (plural) and they limited themselves based on what they cast (Luke 5:1-7). Have faith for the great haul; all is possible with God. My God shall supply all your needs and exceed them (Philippians 4:19); whatever you gave up God returns a hundred-fold. You need to have enough pots, you need to have enough nets, you need to have enough vessels to take in this great haul! Get ready for the haul; stop thinking small minded. God is able to do exceeding abundantly above (Ephesians 3:20); so, think that way. The wealth of the sinner is laid up for you (Proverbs 13:22); go receive it! You have not because you ask not (James 4:2); when you ask, ask in faith believing that He is going to be a rewarder of those that diligently seek Him (Hebrews 11:6). Jesus died that we might live an abundant life (John 10:10); ask for it. God's word gives the promise of prospering and being in good health even as your soul prospers (3 John 2); claim it now. He will even make sure you have enough taxes (Matthew 17:24-27); believe it! The promises of God include the fact that at His right hand are pleasures ever more (Psalm 16:11); so, remain in His presence and seek His face. Because you want all that God has for you on this side of heaven; decide that no good thing will He withhold (Psalm 84:11). Since He isn't withholding from us; you shouldn't withhold any good thing from Him and the blessings will continue.

We have a responsibility to be good stewards over all that He has given us. Let's walk in it.

Lord we thank you for all that you have given us and the tone in which you have given it as well. We ask that you prick our hearts to give as you have decided. You said you love a hilarious giver, you love a cheerful giver. So, tell us what it is that you desire for us to give. And as you continue to prick us, help us then Father to be obedient to your Word. We anticipate that the returns will then be overflowing so that it is obvious to everyone that you have favored us; that you have graced us. We will be so careful to give you all the glory and all the praise. In Jesus' name we do pray and give you thanks. Amen.

> New Testament
> Giving
> Bible Study
> Page 235

Chapter 10: Bible Studies

In God We Trust

Define Trust:

Total surrender to His will
Resting from fleshly labor
Understanding He's working
Seeking His face
Thanking God in advance of the manifestation

What does total surrender mean?

What does it look like in your life?

Resting from fleshly labor puts God in control. Are you resting? What changes should you make?

When we are in crisis or just dealing with the issues of life, God is still working. When you have prayed for divine intervention, stand on the Word and know God is still working. What is God working on for you?

Seeking has the connotation of searching, attempting to find, endeavoring for more, and asking for something from someone. What are you seeking God for and what Scriptural reference backs up your request?

Thanking God for coming through is always appropriate. When we truly trust God, we can thank Him in advance even before the manifestation has presented itself. What are you thankful for?

Money Test

Work Ethic

Read Matthew 20:1-16 (Parable of the workers)

What is your reaction to being underpaid?

How do you react when you feel underpaid?

Is it reasonable?

Do you over react to issues with money? (anger, insomnia, critical, etc.)

Does your work change with your paycheck?

How do you feel about your current pay?

Are you content with your pay?

Have you been offended in this area?

What happened?

Why? (include the part you played)

Have you prayed and asked God to remove the offense? Correct the situation? Give insight to your leader?

Have you forgiven the individual?

Are you ready to forgive now?

If not, why not?

Do you see the prison of bitterness and unforgiveness closing you in?

GET OUT NOW!

Self Control

Read Luke 12:16-21

Where are your priorities? List your top 5 in order.

Is your financial growth ranked higher than your spiritual growth?

Are you selfish? Are you willing to give to others?

Do you spend excessively?

Can you walk by a sale and not purchase?

Do you have a budget?

Do you stick to it?

Do you have consumer debt over $10,000? (credit cards, personal loans, student loans, etc.)

Do you have the generous characteristic like our Father God?

How do you demonstrate it?

Read James 2:1-16

Who have you treated differently?

If you are still treating them differently, what changes are you making and when?

Read Matthew 6:19-21

Are you storing treasure in heaven?

What does it look like to you?

Develop an acronym for TREASURE that is easy for you to remember to look heavenward.

T _____
R _____
E _____
A _____
S _____
U _____
R _____
E _____

Integrity

Read Deuteronomy 23:21-23

What vows/ agreements have you made?

Which have you continued to pay?

Which have you let slip and need to repent and begin paying off? (include all collection agencies, family members, etc.)

Read Psalm 37:21

How does your heart need to change about money and paying debts?

Are you showing mercy to those that owe you?

Are you giving? Where?

Read Psalm 15:4
What does this say to you?

What do you need to finish even though it will cost you more? (even if you agreed to hastily)

Are you manipulative? How?

What actions will you change to stop?

Are you deceptive?

Who can hold you accountable?

Ask them to be your accountability partner and document the date. How often will you check in?

Are you selfish? How?

What action steps are you willing to take to overcome this issue?

Read Galatians 5:22-25

List the Fruit of the Spirit:

Define each:

Are you displaying the Fruit of the Spirit?

What action steps are you committed to take to develop in these areas?

Love for People

Read James 2:17

Can your faith be seen? How?

If not, what steps will you begin to take so that it can be seen?

Read Luke 12:48

What have you been given?

What do you see is required of you?

Read 1 Timothy 5:8

Are you prepared to take care of your family members?

What does that look like to you?

Read 1 Timothy 6:7

If you were to give an account of your stewardship today, are you pleased? Would God be pleased?

Read 1 Timothy 6:17

All things have been given to you to enjoy. Are you enjoying what God has given? How?

Read Luke 16:10-13

What stands out to you?

What do you need to do differently?

What are the true riches?

Read Galatians 6:10

What opportunity has been presented to you to do good?

Over the next weeks, jot down opportunities God created and how you reacted.

How have you considered the leaders in your church? How can you do good to them?

Has your view of their compensation changed?

If so, how?

When it comes to special offering requests, do you move your giving from one bucket to another? (i.e. same total amount just redistributed)

Are you a generous giver?

Who told you that?

Who and what organizations do you give to regularly?

Love for God

How did the cookie illustration affect you?

Can you see God as the older gentleman?

Have you been selfishly consuming all He has given?

How will you act differently?

Read Matthew 22: 1-14

Examine your heart on giving to God and giving to the house of God (storehouse). What comes to mind?

Do you give regularly?

Do you give each time you gather for service?

Read Mark 12:41-44 & Luke 21:1-4

If Jesus watched your last offering, what would He think?

Since He always watches, what will you do differently?

Any change in the amount you should give?

Any change in the emotion behind your giving?

How much more should you be willing to give God?

Abundant Living

Read John 10:10.

Insert your name: I am come that _____ might have life and that _____ might have it more abundantly! (meditate on this promise)

Are you living the abundant life?

Considering the levels poverty and prosperity; where are you?

Why do you consider yourself at that level?

What are you doing to get to a higher level?

What Scripture references promises you more? (write them down and meditate on them)

Read Exodus 16

Identify miracle provisions God showed the children of Israel.

Read Matthew 6

What does God promise?

What are you asking God for?

Read Isaiah 55:8-11

What miraculous things does God do?

Can we always see Him working before the result?

Read Mark 4:26-29

What seeds have you planted that God is working on?

Are you watering those requests with the Word? What Scriptural promise lines up with your request?

Pray these promises!

Coming out of Poverty

Using the definition of poverty, are you at this level?

If not skip this Bible Study and continue with Going onto Abundance.

If your basic needs aren't met, it's time to change your thinking. Read Hebrews 11:6

Do you believe in God?

Do you believe He will reward you?

Look up the definition for seek.

Seek God for answers. Write down your questions.

Are you working?

If not, where can you begin looking for work?

Are there areas in your life that you have given to the enemy? What are they?

Take authority over these areas. Write out Scriptural promises for your basic needs. (Read through the section again to find them)

Read Matthew 18:18-20 until you are fully persuaded of your authority.

Are you returning your tithe? If not, start now.

Read Malachi 3:8-11 and declare God will rebuke the devourer for your sake.

Ask for angels to be dispatched to minister to you.

What Scripture ensures angelic assistance? Write it out.

Practice repeating God's word in prayer. Write out your prayer needs including Scriptural promises.

Ask for Godly wisdom to proceed.

Going onto Abundance

Read the following passages and write your desires based on them.

3 John 2

Joshua 1:7-8

Psalm 35:27

Psalm 1:1-3

Jeremiah 17:7-8

Psalm 112:1-3

Proverbs 10:22

Proverbs 22:4

2 Corinthians 8:9

2 Corinthians 9:8-11

Hebrews 8:6

Psalm 37:25

Psalm 27:13

Jeremiah 31:31-34

Hebrews 9:15

Hebrews 12:24

Scriptural Ways to Achieve Abundance

Favor

Research men and women of favor and describe the favor they received.

Esther

David

Solomon

Samuel

Abraham

Israel

Jacob

Research the richest men in the Bible and what they possessed.

Job

Abraham

Solomon

Meditate on these Scriptures:
Meditate – ponder, revolve around in the minds, speak aloud to oneself.

Proverbs 23:7 *"For as he thinketh in his heart, so is he: Eat and drink, saith he to thee; but his heart is not with thee."*

Whatever tape that you have been running and playing in your mind needs to stop. You know that recording that says something like, "I'm no good, I'm broke busted and disgusted." Change the recording to what God says about you. He said, "I created you to live in abundance. I created you to be a good Steward over what I've given you. If the cattle on a thousand hills are mine and it is according to His riches in glory". His riches reference that it is innumerable and immeasurable. There is no limit to what God is able to do.

Proverbs 11:27 *"He that diligently seeketh good procureth favour: but he that seeketh mischief, it shall come unto him."*

This passage has antithetical parallelism meaning the first portion is directly contradictory to the last half. Seeking God gives us favor. Seeking mischief is a self-fulfilling prophecy.

Galatians 4:7 *"Wherefore thou art no more a servant, but a son; and if a son, then an heir of God through Christ."*

You have a right to whatever that inheritance is whatever was left to you legally is yours. You have the right to walk in it from a vital standpoint.

Romans 8:14-17

Luke 24:49

Acts 1:4

2 Corinthians 3:5,6 AMP *"Not that we are fit (qualified and sufficient in ability) of ourselves to form personal judgments or to claim or count anything as coming from us, but our power and ability and sufficiency are from God. [It is He] Who has qualified us [making us to be fit and worthy and sufficient] as ministers and dispensers of a new covenant [of salvation through Christ], not [ministers] of the letter (of legally written code) but of the Spirit; for the code [of the Law] kills, but the [Holy] Spirit makes alive"*

2 Corinthians 6:1

Ephesians 2:5,6 *"Even when we were dead in sins, hath quickened us together with Christ, (by grace ye are saved;) And hath raised us up together, and made us sit together in heavenly places in Christ Jesus:"*

Favor with God and man is received from God through fellowship and renewing of the mind. The word fellowship is the Greek word *koinonia*. God is going to use man to bless man.

Ephesians 6:21-24 *"But that ye also may know my affairs, and how I do, Tychicus, a beloved brother and faithful minister in the Lord, shall make known to you all things: Whom I have sent unto you for the same purpose, that ye might know our affairs, and that he might comfort your hearts. Peace be to the brethren, and love with faith, from God the Father and the Lord Jesus Christ. Grace be with all them that love our Lord Jesus Christ in sincerity. Amen."*

The Bible records that love must be "in sincerity". You must be genuine not with hypocrisy. We don't have a reason to bless everybody but those that are His we must.

Matthew 6:33 *"But seek ye first the kingdom of God, and his righteousness; and all these things shall be added unto you."*

The word "all" incorporates everything from verse 25. The Bible says all will be added unto you and so favor with God and man is received from God through our fellowship as well as renewing of our mind. As our mind is conformed to God's word (Romans 12:2); we will receive by faith and sowing. We can't just attain by being a reservoir. The attitude that holds is not one that God can funnel blessings through. God will bless you if he knows he can get it through you but if he knows you're going to hold on to it, He won't send it your way. My grandmother passed away in 2004 and she made the best peach cobbler. I was in school at Georgia Tech and she lived in Columbus, Georgia. I would drive there on the weekend since it was about 45 minutes away. My cousin came from Athens (University of Georgia). MaDear (that's what we called my grandmother) made me a peach cobbler and I purposed to take it back to school with me. The entire weekend I kept it in the brown paper bag. Every now and then I would look at it. Before I was ready to leave I peered in the bag and it was molded. My motives were selfish. At her funeral I shared the story and told everybody how she taught me to share. Being a reservoir blocks blessings from others and sometimes limits yours as well.

Matthew 7:7

Matthew 7:9-12

Luke 6:37-38 *"Judge not, and ye shall not be judged: condemn not, and ye shall not be condemned: forgive, and ye shall be forgiven: Give, and it shall be given unto you; good measure, pressed down, and shaken together, and running over, shall men give into your bosom. For with the same measure that ye mete withal it shall be measured to you again."*

What you give out shall be measured to you again. We like to sing this song, "Pressed down shaken together,

running over", it's not talking about money but you can apply it in that manner. Whatever you want in return you need to sow. If you want mercy or forgiveness then you must sow it into others.
Galatians 6:6-10

Isaiah 54:1

Romans 8:28

Romans 8:30

Hebrews 12:2-3 *"Looking unto Jesus the author and finisher of our faith; who for the joy that was set before him endured the cross, despising the shame, and is set down at the right hand of the throne of God. For consider him that endured such contradiction of sinners against himself, lest ye be wearied and faint in your minds."*

We look to God for strength. We also look to what Jesus did and continues to do as our great high priest. There is nothing new under the sun and Jesus has experienced everything we will go through. He knows what we're feeling; He was betrayed, denied, beaten, bruised and rejected. Jesus was kicked when He was down, He can sympathize with us. If we look to what He has already done; He didn't remain on the cross, though it was very difficult His desire was that we be reconciled to God. The Bible lets us know that for the joy that was set before Him; He endured. One day He saw in the future that we would join Him in heaven, one day we will be in the presence of God. The wages of sin is death but Jesus already paid the price. One day He knew He was going to get the keys to the kingdom back for us that we could bind and loose. The joy that was before him was that one day _____ (insert your name) was coming and because you were coming Jesus endured the cross.

In the book of James, he says faith without works is dead so we have to step out on faith and trust God that He will lead us. If we write down our specific need and ask God for favor in that area we have already overcome.

2 Corinthians 3:18

John 16:13-15

John 10:27

Colossians 3:23

Matthew 5:16 *"Let your light so shine before men, that they may see your good works, and glorify your Father which is in heaven."*

Subjunctively, with possibility, they may see your good works and glorify your Father. Do all to the glory of God. Confess to stay in favor

John 6:63

Isaiah 55:10-11

Numbers 20:7-12

Psalm 106:32-33

Mark 11:23-24

Proverbs 18:21 *"Death and life are in the power of the tongue: and they that love it shall eat the fruit thereof."*

The power of life and death is in your tongue. Remember the 5 infallible steps of faith: meditation; illumination; prayer of faith; confession; and possession. The battle is won or lost at confession.

Journal your thoughts:

Covenant

Read the definition of covenant.

What benefits do you have in your covenant with God? List them (see Psalm 34)

What is your tithe? $

Are you in covenant?

Do you have a budget?

If no, create one
If yes, Do you clearly identify tithe and offering?
If not, re-create it

Are you giving your tithe first?

Are you a generous giver?

Pray the prayer at the end of the section on covenant. What is God revealing to you about your giving?

(For more practical applications of budgeting, debt reduction, savings, etc. see Financial Wisdom For Financial Freedom)

Summarizing the Journey

Review the charts and determine where you are.

Is it where you desire to be?

What steps will you take to move along to Canaan?

Write down what God is saying your next steps should be.

Journal your feelings

New Testament Giving

Meditate on the miracle provisions

Ephesians 3:20
Proverbs 13:22
1 Kings 17:1-16
2 Kings 4:1-7
Matthew 17:24-27

Journal your thoughts and how much more you expect a miracle provision.

I'm so excited that you are now a part of the Heart 2 Heart Truth Ministries family! Please share your experience with others and by commenting.

Whether it's coaching for you to go further faster, online courses conveniently moving you forward or books that inspire, encourage and educate... we help you put feet to your faith so you can walk victoriously!

Group study is also encouraged.

https://ChontaHaynes.com
https://H2HTruth.org

YouTube Channel: https://youtube.com/@ChontaHaynes

Podcast: https://www.chontahaynes.com/podcasts/heart-2-heart-truth-empowering-faith-driven-women-and-entrepreneurs-to-walk-in-victory

Facebook:
https://www.facebook.com/chonta.haynes/
https://facebook.com/h2htruth
https://www.facebook.com/groups/tbibletruth
https://www.facebook.com/groups/treasuredwoman

Instagram: https://Instagram.com/ctahaynes

LinkedIn: https://linkedin.com/in/chonta-haynes

Twitter: https://twitter.com/chonta_haynes

Linktree : https://linktr.ee/chontahaynes

TikTok: https://tictok.com/ctahaynes

Heart 2 Heart Truth Foundation 501 (c) 3

God has provided opportunities to meet the needs of others and bring the Gospel in a practical way. Dr. Haynes' books have been distributed through the library system, churches and Christian colleges to serve the larger population.

Donate: https://www.paypal.com/donate?hosted_button_id=UZG5B9KX59U4S

Looking for next steps to gain total financial success?

https://chontahaynes.com/kfscourse
https://chontahaynes.com/coaching
https://chontahaynes.com/destiny

Also available:

Financial Wisdom For Financial Freedom
ISBN 9780999173305
ISBN 9780999173312

Divinely Connected: Steps to Fearless Financial Freedom
ISBN 9780999173343
ISBN 9780999173350

Divinely Connected: Sister 2 Sister
ISBN 9780999173381
ISBN 9781736395905

Divinely Connected: Praying Through Life's Struggles
ISBN 9780999173398
ISBN 9781736395912

Financial Bundle
Heart 2 Heart Truth Ministries
EMPOWERING YOU TO PUT FEET TO YOUR FAITH AND WALK VICTORIOUSLY!
ChontaHaynes.com/bundles

Taking you on a journey to transform your finances

PICK UP OR DOWNLOAD YOUR COPY TODAY!
https://ChontaHaynes.com/bundles

Leader Kits also available:
https://chontahaynes.com/leader

ONLINE COURSES

https://chontahaynes.com/courses

Courses designed to guide you to the next level at your pace and when you are ready.

REGISTER TODAY!
https://chontahaynes.com/courses

God's Blueprint for Your Finances

A transformational course that helps you manage your money, grow your wealth, and fulfill your calling—without compromising your faith.

START TODAY!

Kingdom Financial Success Course:
https://chontahaynes.com/kfscourse

ABOUT THE AUTHOR

Dr. Chonta T. A. Haynes
Author * Speaker * Coach
CEO, Heart 2 Heart Truth Ministries
Https://ChontaHaynes.com
https://youtube.com/c/chontahaynes

Dr. Chonta T. A. Haynes empowers women to confidently live life with peace and financial security. Through her Amazon Best Selling books, coaching programs and Keynotes, she equips with Biblically based resources. From her experience and degrees in engineering, theology and Christian counseling she balances logic and faith. Known as the **Destiny Designer, Performance Excellence Transition Coach** and **Biblical Money Management expert**, she simplifies complex problems and creates actionable and effective solutions with sustainable results. To succeed in these challenging times, individuals and organizations turn to Dr. Chonta to provide strategies that work. As CEO and Founder of Heart 2 Heart Truth Ministries and Heart 2 Heart Truth Foundation her mission is to help you put feet to your faith so that you can walk victoriously.

Dr. Haynes, The Destiny Designer™—empowers purpose-driven leaders to walk boldly in identity, cultivate sustainable impact, and steward unstoppable success across faith, family, and future generations

With a strong foundation in **business development** and **strategic empowerment**, she helps clients move from clarity to action—bridging the gap between where they are and where they were destined to be. Her mission is to guide high-capacity individuals and visionary teams to not only discover their purpose but to build profitable, principle-based platforms that thrive

Whether you're navigating transition, scaling your vision, or seeking greater **financial freedom**, she offers frameworks and strategies that produce tangible outcomes, sustainable growth, and kingdom-minded impact.

Helping you put feet to your faith so you can walk victoriously!

https://linktr.ee/chontahaynes

www.ingramcontent.com/pod-product-compliance
Lightning Source LLC
Chambersburg PA
CBHW070543010526
44118CB00012B/1200